# NIGHT

## NOTES

*including*
- *Life and Background*
- *Elie Wiesel's Published Works*
- *A Brief Synopsis*
- *List of Characters*
- *Historical Timeline*
- *Critical Commentaries*
- *Map*
- *Genealogy*
- *Critical Essays*
    Wiesel and the Critics
    Autobiography and History
    The Focus on "Night" as a Symbol
    Elie Wiesel and Mysticism
    Elie Wiesel and Existentialism
    Elie Wiesel and the Wandering Jew
    The Theme of Faith
    The State of Israel
    Literary Devices
    A Note on Translation
- *Review Questions and Essay Topics*
- *Selected Bibliography*
- *Historical Background*

*by*
*Maryam Riess, M.A.*
*University of North Carolina at Greensboro*

INCORPORATED

**Editor**

Gary Carey, M.A.
University of Colorado

**Consulting Editor**

James L. Roberts, Ph.D.
Department of English
University of Nebraska

ISBN 0-8220-0893-9
© Copyright 1996
by
**Hungry Minds, Inc.**
909 Third Avenue
New York, NY 10022
All Rights Reserved
Printed in U.S.A.

Graphics by Raymond M. Barrett, Jr.

# CONTENTS

# NIGHT

## Notes

### LIFE AND BACKGROUND

Each era of turmoil tends to suffuse with truth a representative spokesperson, a survivor who is thrust into the light by the Zeitgeist, the metaphoric "spirit of the times." The looming evil of Hitler's Third Reich produced a slight, solitary, sad-eyed stoic with the number A-7713 tattooed on his left arm. He came of age after World War II among orphans belonging to no country. He learned the journalist's trade and delivered to an uncaring, bigoted, cyclically vicious world a denunciation of gratuitous murder: "Never again!"

Dr. Elie Wiesel (**eh** lee wee **zehl**), noted proponent of peace and reconciliation, pioneered single-author Holocaust literature based on eyewitness accounts. As a leading American advocate of memorials and reclamation of Holocaust memorabilia, he has published a forceful stream of speeches, polemics, autobiography, drama, fiction, documentary, and articles. Driven by an empathy that impels him to protest carnage and to impose humanitarian values on behalf of the world's oppressed, he has heeded an inner compulsion to serve humanity by illuminating the hate-darkened past.

**Early Years.** The world's most renowned writer of Holocaust literature, Eliezer "Elie" Wiesel seems forever on the cusp between devout Jew and agnostic existentialist. From his pen pour the repeated *why*'s, a demand for response from the silent God whom Elie revered from childhood as the guiding figure of his being. The grandson of rabbis and only son and third of four children of grocers Shlomo (spelled "Chlomo" in *Night*) and Sarah Feig Wiesel, he was born September 30, 1928, in the *shtetl*, or village, of Sighet, Romania, in the Carpathian Mountains, a thriving Judaic cultural center for 15,000 Jews which was later absorbed by Hungary. Shy, somber-eyed, and introspective at age three, Elie attended classes under a revered rabbi and learned the Hebrew alphabet, recalling in later years the simple classroom repetition of *aleph, beth, gimel* (A, B, C). A scholarly child, he preferred chess to soccer and followed the orthodox Hasidic traditions by wearing *peyes*, or side curls, and donning tefillin, the traditional leather phylacteries that bound scripture to his forehead and arm before morning prayers; on Fridays, he honored the Sabbath with prayers, meditation, devotional readings, and chants. He picked apricots on his grandfather's farm, was blessed at age eight by the revered Rabbi Israel of Wizhnitz, challenged friend Itzu Goldblatt in a match of piety and self-discipline, and attended high school in Debrecen and Nagyvárad with the intention of becoming a writer.

Wiesel had superb role models. His maternal grandfather, Dodye Feig, a white-bearded farmer, told lively stories and shared the camaraderie of the family prodigy, who, in early childhood, was obviously preparing for a life of piety and scholarship. Elie's father, a shopkeeper and revered community leader and counselor, served the town as a mediator for Jews and a saintly humanitarian to the needy. Himself a victim of torture and jail for aiding Jews to escape persecution in Poland, Shlomo urged Elie to trust in human goodness and to study modern Hebrew, Freudian psychology, and astronomy. In contrast to Shlomo's aims for his contemplative son, Wiesel's mother, a high school graduate who was the voice of tradition throughout his childhood, quoted Goethe and Schiller and guided him toward traditional Judaism through study of the Torah, Talmud, and cabbala, the Hasidic mystical lore that he studied with Moshe the Beadle, a synagogue caretaker. While Elie entered his teens and studied for a life of orthodoxy, Nazi soldiers under the command of Reichsführer Heinrich Himmler were introducing the deadly poisonous Zyklon B to death camps, where they efficiently gassed exiles from Russia, Silesia, Bohemia, and Moravia in large numbers before disposing of their remains in camp crematories.

**The War Years.** The German high command moved closer during the celebration of Purim on March 19, 1944, and put the Hungarian police in charge of the "Jewish problem," which included all people with Jewish surnames, even those who had converted to Christianity or who had never practiced the Jewish faith. By Passover, local police, goaded by the fascist Nyilas party, began imposing the Nuremberg Laws:

- closing Jewish-owned shops and offices
- desecrating and looting synagogues
- conducting raids and inspections of "sanitary measures"
- outlawing marriage between Jews and Gentiles
- imposing a three-day curfew
- posting warnings of potential execution for noncompliance.

The purported reason for mass anti-Semitism was to put down a "Jewish conspiracy," a nonexistent plot that Hitler claimed threatened all Europe. In May 1944, when Russian troops were twelve miles from Sighet, Adolf Hitler's master plan called for storm troopers to load convoys to hasten the removal and annihilation of Romania's "undesirables"—trade unionists, Jehovah's Witnesses, Catholics, Jews, Gypsies, retardates, homosexuals, the elderly, and the physically handicapped, blind, and deaf. Elie's father joined the council of elders and Gestapo officers in a discussion of the future for Jews of Sighet. As storm troopers began stringing barbed wire around the Jewish ghetto, local doctors learned of a village annihilation plot and several committed suicide before the massive assault left them no choice.

Elie's family had fleeting opportunities to escape deportation. A compassionate police officer tapped at their window to warn them of danger. On May 14, Eli's father refused an offer of safe refuge in a cabin in the mountains from Maria, his Christian housekeeper, who lived on the outskirts of town. Two days later, authorities resituated Elie's family in Uncle Mendel's house in the smaller of two ghettos, then later transported them aboard the last rail convoy. In a sealed cattle car they traveled to Birkenau, the SS sorting center for the infamous Auschwitz complex, where guards tossed babies into flaming ditches. During their banishment, Elie dreamed noble reveries of Jews in antiquity and contemplated the romance of exile. As he neared the burning ditch, however, he feared that his life was about to end in a burst of flame. By the end of the war, his romantic notions of martyrdom crumbled along with the remains of six million Jewish corpses. The Jewish population of his homeland had been reduced by half.

In *Night* (1960) and *All Rivers Run to the Sea* (1995), Wiesel details camp life and the caprices of fate that saved ten to fifteen percent for enforced labor and destroyed others, sometimes whole convoys. After a midnight arrival, he joined his father in the men's line; his mother and sisters followed the women to separate confines. Sarah Wiesel and her youngest, Tzipora, apparently died in the Birkenau ovens; his older sisters survived. (Note: Wiesel avoids describing the ordeals of his sisters, which he considers private matters.) During idle moments in camp, he prayed, performed daily rituals, and recited from the Torah and Talmud. Dressed in shapeless striped prison garb, cap, and clogs at Auschwitz II, he and his father endured hard labor, cold, malnutrition, and arbitrary lashings. Barracks conditions were primitive and provided only skimpy straw or excelsior bedding on wooden slats and a night bucket for a toilet. Poor sanitation and a lack of soap and pure water spread intestinal bacteria, vermin, typhus, and cholera.

Upon transfer to Auschwitz III, the electrical warehouse at Buna, south of the Vistula River, father and son sorted electrical parts until Elie entered a camp infirmary in January 1945 for surgery to relieve an inflamed foot. (In *All Rivers Run to the Sea*, Wiesel describes the infirmity as a swollen knee.) On January 18, the threat of Russian troops forced the Germans to mount a chaotic camp evacuation forty-two miles on foot to Gleiwitz, Poland, to board roofless cattle cars for a ten-day journey northwest to Buchenwald in central Germany. There, two and a half months before American forces liberated the camp, Shlomo Wiesel died of dysentery, malnutrition, and a blow to the head, leaving his son to doubt God's existence and to mourn with the little strength he had left.

**Liberation.**    On April 11, Allied liberators arrived to feed and tend the starving survivors. Elie was so ill that he collapsed and was treated at the former SS hospital. No list of survivors named his parents or sisters. At the invitation of Charles de Gaulle, the *Oeuvre au Secours aux Enfants* (Children's Rescue Service) shuttled Elie by train along with four hundred fellow orphans to Belgium, then to a château at Écouis, Normandy, for recuperation. Because he misunderstood a border guard's spoken offer of French citizenship, he remained stateless. In June, he began a journal in Yiddish, his native language. He reunited with his older sister Hilda and learned that Beatrice had returned to Sighet; the three later met at Antwerp. In 1948, because he had no kinship ties with citizens of the new state of Israel, a rejection for a visa to Palestine ended his ambition of becoming a freedom fighter for Haganah, the Zionist underground.

Without making a clear choice of careers, in 1948 Wiesel

enrolled in literature and philosophy courses at the Sorbonne in Paris and heard lectures by novelist Jean-Paul Sartre and philosopher Martin Buber. To better interpret wartime trauma and SS evil, he studied asceticism with the mystic specialist Shushani, but vowed not to write about his experiences. Often suicidal and hungry on the meager stipend of $16 per month, he lingered at the orphanage and contemplated alternatives while healing his spirit from the aftereffects of rootlessness and trauma. He worked part-time as tutor, director of a choir of displaced persons, movie subtitler, camp counselor, and translator for the militant Yiddish weekly *Zion in Kamf* before accepting a post as a multilingual journalist for the Yiddish weekly *Yedioth Ahronoth*.

**Wiesel the Writer.** On May 14, 1955, François Mauriac, Nobel-prize winning French novelist and biographer of General Charles de Gaulle, encouraged Wiesel to speak for the survivors of the Holocaust. Mauriac advised Wiesel on the publication of *Night*, a humanistic documentary which the author and his publisher pared down from a more than 800-page *Un di Velt Hot Geshvign* (And the World Remained Silent) to a manuscript one-eighth of the original, a spare, intense first-person account of his incarceration by the Nazi SS. The book was translated from Yiddish into French, retitled *La Nuit*, and dedicated to his parents and his little sister. It garnered weak response from potential publishers, who doubted that so pessimistic a story would find a ready audience. Meanwhile, Wiesel's journalistic career took him to Spain, Tangiers, Morocco, eastern Europe, Canada, Brazil, India, and Israel, where he observed the early years of Jewish statehood. While translating for the World Jewish Conference in Geneva, he followed the emergence of David Ben-Gurion, the bold Israeli leader, and met the great political, philosophical, and military figures of the era: General Moshe Dayan, Hannah Arendt, Pierre Mendès-France, Golda Meir, Nikita Khrushchev, Sir Anthony Eden, General Dwight Eisenhower, and Marshal Georgy Zhukov.

After moving to the United States in 1956, Wiesel lived alone at a hotel and wrote a spy novel under the pseudonym Elisha Carmeli while he reported U. N. activities for the *Morgen Journal*, a popular newspaper for immigrant Jews. In July of that year, he was hit by a speeding taxi in the heart of New York City. The first hospital where he was taken rejected him because he was considered too poor and not likely to recover. His injuries put him in a full-body cast and confined him to a wheelchair for a year. During his lengthy recuperation, he applied for United States citizenship, which he finally received in 1963.

On April 2, 1969, in the Ramban synagogue in the old sector of Jerusalem, Wiesel married Austrian-born writer and editor Marion Erster Rose, a survivor of the Holocaust and mother of a daughter named Jennifer. Wiesel lives in New York with his wife and their son, Shlomo Elisha, born in 1972, now a Yale graduate specializing in computer science. Currently, Marion oversees the translation of her husband's works and joins with him in overseeing work of the Wiesel Foundation for Humanity, a consortium that studies the source and impetus of hate groups.

**Wiesel the Humanitarian.** A prolific writer and speaker, Wiesel appeals to a wide audience of young Jews who, in the 1960s, felt cut off from their traditions and their ancestors' struggles. The receipts from his lectures he gives to a yeshiva, an Orthodox Jewish school; his book royalties he donates to a fund for a synagogue to honor his father, whose death so near liberation continues to haunt Wiesel. He supports Holocaust survivors, lectures, publishes, and comments on the subjects of world indifference to suffering, Cambodian refugees, the Vietnamese "boat people," the "disappeared" of Argentina, Arab refugees in Palestine, and nuclear proliferation. He attended the Adolf Eichmann trial in 1961 and the Jewish liberation of Jerusalem, filmed a visit to Sighet for NBC twenty years after his deportation, and in 1965 risked arrest in a Moscow airport while visiting Russian Jewish "refuseniks." He sympathized with Martin Luther King's civil rights efforts, rebuked former President Reagan in 1985 for honoring the Bitburg Cemetery for SS corpsmen, and bolsters humanitarian efforts in Biafra, Northern Ireland, Yugoslavia, and Bosnia. In 1987, he testified about his experiences at Auschwitz during the trial of war criminal Klaus Barbie in Lyons, France.

A classroom influence for human rights, Wiesel, formerly Distinguished Professor of Judaic Studies at Manhattan's City College of New York, has served Yale and Florida International universities as a visiting scholar. He has remained at Boston University since 1976 as the Andrew Mellon Professor of Humanities. Named chairman of the U.S. Holocaust Memorial Council by President Jimmy

Carter, Wiesel is often called upon as a consultant and receives continual publicity and acclaim for his insistent illumination of the Holocaust, which he considers a holy event, and his denunciation of the bystanders who witnessed the loading of cattle cars and made no outcry. His honors include the American Liberties Medallion, Prix Médicis, Prix Rivarol, Prix de l'Universalité, Joseph Prize for Human Rights, Eleanor Roosevelt Memorial, Martin Luther King, Jr. Medallion, Raoul Wallenberg Medal, and, in 1985, the Congressional Gold Medal of Achievement. His honorary degrees derive from a broad span of colleges and universities: Jewish Theological Seminary, Hebrew Union, Manhattanville, Yeshiva, Boston, Spertus College of Judaica, Wesleyan, Notre Dame, Anna Maria, Brandeis, Bar-Ilan, Hofstra, Talmudic, Marquette, Simmons, St. Scholastica, Tufts, Moravian, Loyola, Emory, and Yale. On December 10, 1986, his sister Hilda attended the Nobel ceremonies at the University of Oslo, Norway, and heard her brother's acceptance of the Peace Prize, an award to a beloved freedom fighter which carried a stipend of $287,769.78 along with the admiration of the civilized world. In 1995, he wrote again of his family's catastrophe and cited events leading up to his marriage in *All Rivers Run to the Sea*, the first volume of a two-part autobiography.

## ELIE WIESEL'S PUBLISHED WORKS

### FICTION

*The Town Beyond the Wall* (1964)
*The Gates of the Forest* (1966)
*A Beggar in Jerusalem* (1970)
*The Oath* (1973)
*The Golem: The Story of a Legend as Told by Elie Wiesel* (1983)
*The Fifth Son* (1985)
*The Forgotten* (1992)

### AUTOBIOGRAPHY/NONFICTION

*Night* (1960)
*Dawn* (1961)
*The Accident* (1962)
*The Jews of Silence: A Personal Report on Soviet Jewry* (1966)
*Legends of Our Time* (1968)

*One Generation After* (1970)
*Souls on Fire: Portraits and Legends of Hasidic Masters* (1972)
*Messengers of God: Biblical Portraits and Legends* (1976)
*Dimensions of the Holocaust* (contributor, 1977)
*Four Hasidic Masters and Their Struggle Against Melancholy* (1978)
*A Jew Today* (1978)
*Dimensions of the Holocaust* (1978)
*Images from the Bible* (art by Shalom of Safed, 1980)
*The Testament* (1981)
*Five Biblical Portraits* (1981)
*Paroles d'étranger* (A Stranger's Words) (1982)
*Somewhere a Master: Further Tales of the Hasidic Masters* (1984)
*Against Silence: The Voice and Vision of Elie Wiesel* (1985)
*Signes d'exode* (Marks of the Exodus) (1985)
*Job, Or God in the Tempest* (1986)
*Twilight* (1988)
*The Six Days of Destruction* (1989)
*Evil and Exile* (with Philippe-Michael de Saint-Cheron, 1990)
*From the Kingdom of Memory* (1990)
*All Rivers Run to the Sea* (1995)

## CASSETTE

"The Accident" (read by George Guidall, Macmillan)
*Elie Wiesel: On Remembering* (National Public Radio)
*Elie Wiesel Reads* Night (excerpts, Spoken Arts)
*Night* (read by Elie Wiesel, Harper-Caedmon)

## CANTATA

*Ani Maanin: A Song Lost and Found Again* (music by Darius
   Milhaud, 1974)

## VIDEO

*Elie Wiesel's Jerusalem* (Coronet, 1978)
*Facing Hate* (discussion with Bill Moyers, PBS, 1991)

## DRAMA

*Zalmen, or the Madness of God* (1968)
*The Trial of God: A Play in Three Acts* (1979)

## ARTICLES AND ESSAYS

"Wiesel's Speech at Nobel Ceremony," *New York Times*, December 11, 1986, A12

"Was He Normal? Human? Poor Humanity," *Time*, May 11, 1987, 93–94

"What Really Makes Us Free," *Parade*, December 27, 1987, 6–8

"A Mideast Peace: Is It Impossible?" *New York Times*, June 23, 1988, A23

"When You Hate, You Become a Prisoner," *USA Today*, October 9, 1990, 12–13

"When Passion Is Dangerous," *Parade*, April 19, 1992, 20–21

"Cry Out Against the Injustice in Yugoslavia," *USA Today*, December 22, 1992, A9

"Have You Learned the Most Important Lesson of All?" *Parade*, May 24, 1992, 4–5

"The Evil at the Dragon's feet," *Time*, June 19, 1995, 66

"The Decision," *Parade*, August 27, 1995, 4–6

"How America and I Chose Each Other," *Parade*, November 5, 1995, 4–5

## A BRIEF SYNOPSIS

In 1944 in the village of Sighet, Romania, twelve-year-old Elie Wiesel spends much time and emotion on the Talmud and on Jewish mysticism. His instructor, Moshe the Beadle, returns from a near-death experience and warns that Nazi aggressors will soon threaten the serenity of their lives. However, even when anti-Semitic measures force the Sighet Jews into supervised ghettos, Elie's family remains calm and compliant. In spring, authorities begin shipping trainloads of Jews to the Auschwitz-Birkenau complex. Elie's family is part of the final convoy. In a cattle car, eighty villagers can scarcely move and have to survive on minimal food and water. One of the deportees, Madame Schächter, becomes hysterical with visions of flames and furnaces.

At midnight on the third day of their deportation, the group looks in horror at flames rising above huge ovens and gags at the stench of burning flesh. Guards wielding billy clubs force Elie's group through a selection of those fit to work and those who face a grim and improbable future. Elie and his father Chlomo lie about their ages and depart with other hardy men to Auschwitz, a concentration camp. Elie's mother and three sisters disappear into Birkenau, the death camp. After viewing infants being tossed in a burning pit, Elie rebels against God, who remains silent. Every day, Elie and Chlomo struggle to keep their health so they can remain in the work force. Sadistic guards and trustees exact capricious punishments. After three weeks, Elie and his father are forced to march to Buna, a factory in the Auschwitz complex, where they sort electrical parts in an electronics warehouse. The savagery reaches its height when the guards hang a childlike thirteen year old, who dies slowly before Elie's eyes.

Despairing, Elie grows morose during Rosh Hashanah services. At the next selection, the doctor culls Chlomo from abler men. Chlomo, however, passes a second physical exam and is given another chance to live. Elie undergoes surgery on his foot.

Because Russian liberation forces are moving ever closer to the Nazi camp, SS troops evacuate Buna in January 1945. The Wiesels and their fellow prisoners are forced to run through a snowy night in bitter cold over a forty-two mile route to Gleiwitz. Elie binds his bleeding foot in strips of blanket. Inmates who falter are shot. Elie prays for strength to save his father from death. At a makeshift barracks, survivors pile together. Three days later, living on mouthfuls of snow, the remaining inmates travel in open cattle cars on a ten-day train ride to Buchenwald in central Germany. Finally, only the Wiesels and ten others cling to life.

In wooden bunks, Elie tries to nurse his father back to health. Gradually, the dying man succumbs to dysentery, malnutrition, and a vicious beating. Elie's mind slips into semi-delirium. When he awakens, Chlomo is gone. Elie fears that he was sent to the ovens while he was still breathing. Resistance breaks out in Buchenwald. In April, American forces liberate the camp. Elie is so depleted by food poisoning that he stares at himself in a mirror and sees the reflection of a corpse.

## LIST OF CHARACTERS

### Eliezer "Elie" Wiesel

An introspective teenager, Elie first begins to hate when Hungarian police strike out with billy clubs and force Jews from their homes. At Auschwitz's Block 17, he berates himself for being a spoiled child and rejecting his first plate of prison soup. He redeems himself by multiple acts of kindness, such as giving up his gold dental crown to spare his father torment for marching out of step. At the end of his incarceration, an emaciated, demoralized Elie bears little resemblance to the teenage boy who left Sighet.

### Chlomo Wiesel

An esteemed grocer, adviser, and religious leader in the village of Sighet, Chlomo is cultured, but realistic. His dedication to others is evident in his accompaniment of the first convoy of deportees to the gates of the ghetto. At the Birkenau ditch where infants are burned, he wishes that Elie had gone with his mother. Elie assumes that his father does not want to witness the murder of his only son.

### Mrs. Wiesel

Elie's mother remains silent and casts questioning looks at her family as she cooks food for the departure from their Sighet home. As the family marches from the large ghetto, her face is expressionless. In Elie's last view of her, she is stroking Tzipora's hair in a reassuring gesture.

### Hilda Wiesel

As she nears the time of betrothal, Elie's oldest sister works in the family store.

### Beatrice "Béa" Wiesel

The second child of the Wiesels, Béa also assists in the family grocery store.

### Tzipora Wiesel

A miniature vision of stoicism during the march to the cattle car, Elie's seven-year-old sister wears a red coat and struggles without complaint under the heavy load she must carry.

### Batya Reich

A relative who lives with the Wiesels in the larger ghetto, Batya hears ominous knocking on a window overlooking the street.

## Stein of Antwerp

A shrunken, bespectacled fellow, Stein introduces himself to Elie's father on the sixth day at Auschwitz. He asks for news of Reizel and their boys, who emigrated to Belgium. In exchange for Elie's fabricated news, the exuberant Stein returns with half rations of bread. The receipt of real news of his family ends his brief fantasy that they thrive in Antwerp.

## Moshe the Beadle

Elie's mentor is an awkward, silent, hesitant man whose pious chanting and dreamy eyes suit the needs of a boy seeking to know more about Jewish mysticism. The synagogue's handyman, Moshe deliberately seeks anonymity among villagers, yet opens himself to an intimate friendship with Elie, whose tearful prayers alert Moshe to the boy's spiritual hunger. After escaping the Gestapo in Poland near the end of 1942, he considers himself a messenger, but the villagers believe he has lost his mind and ignore his frenzied warning. (Note: Moshe's manic sobbing and subsequent withdrawal are symptomatic of a mental disorder currently known as post-traumatic shock syndrome, a common state of emotional dysfunction that affects survivors of war, terrorism, kidnapping, or other threats to safety or well-being.)

## Berkovitz

A villager who returns from Budapest, Berkovitz reports that Fascists are terrorizing Hungarian Jews.

## Madame Kahn

The Wiesels' neighbor, she provides temporary housing to a polite German officer who buys her a box of chocolates.

## Stern

A thin Sighet police officer, Stern summons Chlomo to a council meeting. At Birkenau, Stern receives an oversized tunic in the chaotic allotment of prison clothing.

## The Hungarian Police Inspector

An unnamed friend, the officer promises to warn Elie's father if danger approaches and knocks on the window early on the morning of the deportation.

## Maria

The Wiesels' servant, Maria pleads with them to leave the unguarded ghetto and seek safety with her.

## Madame Schächter

A quiet fifty-year-old deportee whose husband and two sons were carried on an earlier convoy, Madame Schächter is left with a ten-year-old son. Her manic state progresses from moans to hysterical cries of "Fire! A terrible fire! Mercy! Oh, that fire!"

## Bela Katz

The son of a Sighet tradesman, Bela is selected to load the crematory and ordered to put his father's corpse into a crematory oven.

## Yechiel

The brother of Sighet's rabbi who, on the night that Elie arrives at Birkenau, weeps for their doom.

## Akiba Drumer

A deep-voiced singer who stirs the hearts of inmates with Hasidic melodies sung at bedtime, Drumer applies cabbalistic numerology to scripture and predicts deliverance from Buna within weeks. After the selection at Block 36, he departs in despair, his faith destroyed. His fellow inmates forget his parting request for a Kaddish.

## Juliek

A bespectacled Polish musician in Buna's orchestra block, Juliek smiles cynically at Elie. Later, he shares crucial information about Idek, the manic Kapo, and, in the dark barracks at Gleiwitz, Juliek gives a final performance from a Beethoven concerto, a violinist's blessing. The next morning, he is dead and his violin trampled.

## Louis

A distinguished Dutch violinist in the orchestra block, Louis complains because Jews are not allowed to play Beethoven's music.

## Hans

A Berlin musician in the orchestra block, he eases Elie's concern about his assignment to the electrical warehouse.

## Franek

A former student from Warsaw who plays in the orchestra block and serves as foreman of the electrical warehouse, Franek keeps Elie near his father while they work, then drops his friendly treatment by demanding Elie's gold dental crown. Franek's willingness to torment Elie's father suggests that the foreman has lost his humanity in the daily supervision of inmates.

## Yossi and Tibi

Czech brothers who work at the electrical warehouse after their parents are killed at Birkenau, Yossi and Tibi are Zionists who befriend Elie and hum Jewish melodies as they dream of immigrating to Palestine. When Block 36 undergoes selection, the brothers join Elie in a successful dash past Dr. Mengele's life-or-death assessing eyes.

## Alphonse

A German Jew who heads the musicians' block, Alphonse devotes himself to providing extra cauldrons of soup for the young and the weak.

## The French Jewess

A fearful worker in the electrical warehouse, the French Jewess pretends to be Aryan by forging papers and speaking only French. She soothes Elie after a severe beating by slipping him a piece of bread, wiping his bloody forehead, and whispering comforting words in German.

## The Young Thief from Warsaw

A sturdy young man; when he is on the gallows, he praises liberty and curses Germany.

### Dutch Oberkapo of the 52nd Cable Unit

A kindly overseer, the Dutch Oberkapo is accused of sabotage. After weeks of torture for stockpiling arms and blowing up Buna's power station, the man refuses to name co-conspirators and is transfered to Auschwitz and never seen again.

### The *Pipel*

A thirteen-year-old assistant to the Dutch Oberkapo, the small, angelic-looking *pipel* is tortured and hanged by slow strangulation because his body is too light to end the execution with one quick snap of the neck.

### Elie's *Blockaelteste*

A veteran of concentration camps and slaughterhouses since 1933, the *Blockaelteste* advises internees on how to deal with fear and pass the selection process.

### The Rabbi from a Little Town in Poland

A devout student of the Talmud, the Polish rabbi concludes that God has no mercy for internees.

### The Hospitalized Hungarian Jew

A ghastly patient wracked by dysentery and certain that he will not pass the next selection, he lies in the bed next to Elie's and believes that Hitler will keep his promise to annihilate all Jews before the war ends.

### The Jewish Doctor

Elie's Jewish physician treats him gently, relieves the swelling in his foot, and promises complete recovery in two weeks.

### Zalman

A worker in the electrical warehouse whose immersion in the Talmud helps him escape reality; he cringes with intestinal cramps on the flight from Buna and sinks down to relieve his bowels. Elie assumes that Zalman is trampled by the inmates rather than shot by the SS.

## Rabbi Eliahou

An aged Polish holy man, like one of the biblical prophets, Rabbi Eliahou maintains a sweet expression and a comforting ministry among others in the camps.

## Eliahou's Son

A disloyal young man, Eliahou's son terrifies Elie by his behavior. Rushing farther ahead than Rabbi Eliahou can manage, the son soon distances himself from the weakening old man, whose stumbling steps threaten to get them both shot as stragglers.

## Meir

A ravenous son who kills his father for a crust of bread. Meir dies when others attack him and grab the stolen bread.

## Meir Katz

A tall, robust gardener at Buna, Meir Katz is a friend of Elie's father. When an unidentified attacker tries to strangle Elie, his father calls on Meir Katz for help. Meir loses hope on the train ride to Gleiwitz when he recalls his son's selection for the crematories.

## Dr. Josef Mengele

A cruel-faced SS officer, Dr. Mengele is armed with a military baton and wears a monocle as he conducts the methodical selection and selects all those too weak to work.

## Idek

The crazed Kapo of the Buna warehouse, Idek appears to have no control over fits of violence.

## The Dentist from Czechoslovakia

A predator who is hanged for enriching himself by collecting gold teeth, the Czech dentist tries to talk Elie out of his gold crown.

## The Dentist from Warsaw

A pawn of Franek, the Polish dentist pulls Elie's crown in the lavatory using a rusty spoon as an extractor.

# HISTORICAL TIMELINE

- **1928**
  **September 30**  Elie Wiesel is born in Sighet, Romania, which later becomes Hungarian territory.

- **1930**
  **January**  Brown-shirted storm troopers murder eight Berlin Jews.
  **October**  Nazis hold 107 seats in the *Reichstag*, Germany's parliament.

- **1933**
  **January**  Hitler becomes Chancellor of Germany.
  **March**  Hitler rises to dictator and withdraws Germany from the League of Nations. Heinrich Himmler establishes Dachau outside Munich, Germany, as the first Nazi death camp; thousands of Jews are murdered here, some in brutal medical experiments.
  **April**  All Jews working in government jobs or teaching in universities are fired.
  **July**  The Nazi party is formally declared to be the only political party in Germany.

- **1935**
  **September**  Nuremberg Laws revoke Jewish citizenship and ban intermarriage with Gentiles.

- **1936**
  **October**  Germany allies with Italy and Japan.

- **1937**
  **July**  Buchenwald concentration camp begins receiving convoys.

- **1938**
  **March**  Germany controls Austria.
  **Early Summer**  Romanian fascists strip Jews of citizenship.
  **October**  Hitler evicts German Jews from their homes and forces them into ghettos.
  **November 9–10**  Nazis carry out a devastating plan called *Kristallnacht* (literally, "Crystal Night," or the Night of Broken Glass), which destroys 7500 Jewish-owned stores and syna-

gogues. Jewish children are banned from German schools. Twenty thousand Jews are taken into "protective custody" and sent to concentration camps. Many Jews emigrate.

- **1939**

  **January**   Hitler reveals his intention to annihilate the Jewish race.

  **March**   Hitler captures the remainder of Czechoslovakia.

  **August**   Germany and Russia enter a ten-year nonaggression pact.

  **September**   Germany precipitates World War II by invading Poland.

- **1940**

  **April**   Germany overruns Norway and Denmark. Auschwitz, Poland, becomes a concentration camp.

  **June**   Germany overruns France.

  **August**   Nazis confine Jews to ghettos.

  **October–November**   Romanian Nazis confiscate Jewish homes, farms, and businesses.

- **1941**

  **January**   Nazis massacre 170 Jews in Bucharest.

  **June**   Nazis shoot 212,000 Romanians. Germany attacks Russia.

  **September**   Himmler uses Zyklon B at Auschwitz. Nazis machine-gun more than 33,000 Jews at Babi Yar, near Kiev, Russia.

  **October 15**   Nazis declare Jews outlaws.

  **December 7**   Japan bombs Pearl Harbor. Hitler declares war on the United States.

  **December 8**   Chelmo is the first death camp to use mobile annihilation vans.

  **Late December**   Twelve-year-old Elie Wiesel meets Moshe the Beadle.

- **1942**

  **Late in the year**   Moshe the Beadle escapes Gestapo slaughter to warn the Jews in Sighet. Nazis transport 200,000 Jews to Trans-Dniestria, in the southwestern Ukraine. Two-thirds die of hunger and disease; others depart for Palestine.

- **1943**
  **March**  Crematories open at Auschwitz.
  **April**  The Warsaw ghetto rebels against the Nazis.
  **July**  Mussolini's government collapses. Allies pursue Nazis into Italy.
- **1944**
  **March**  Adolf Eichmann supervises the deportation of Hungarian Jews.
  **April**  Nazis arrest Jewish leaders and close synagogues in Sighet. Jews are quarantined. Nazis confiscate valuables and force Sighet Jews to wear the yellow Star of David and ban them from restaurants, cafes, and public transportation.
  **May 16**  All Sighet Jews are forced from their homes and told to line up in the street at 8 A.M. At 1 P.M., the first group departs by train.
  **Several days later**  Elie's family marches to the "little ghetto."
  **A few days later**  The Wiesels join the last group of deportees aboard a railway cattle car.
  **Late May**  The convoy reaches Birkenau, and Elie and Chlomo spend their first night in camp.
  **Summer**  Guards send Elie and Chlomo to Auschwitz. There, they meet Stein of Antwerp. Elie and Chlomo march to Buna. Elie is tattooed A-7713 on his left arm.
  **July 20**  Colonel Claus von Stauffenberg attempts to murder Hitler.
  **August 25**  The Allies liberate Paris.
  **October 26**  Himmler dismantles the Auschwitz crematory.
- **1945**
  **January**  Elie undergoes surgery in the Auschwitz infirmary. Chlomo and Elie run with evacuees to Gleiwitz, where they and others board open cattle cars for a ten-day ride to Buchenwald in central Germany.
  **January 18**  The Red Army liberates Auschwitz.
  **Late January**  Chlomo Wiesel dies in a bunk at Buchenwald.
  **February**  Franklin Roosevelt, Winston Churchill, and Joseph Stalin meet at Yalta to discuss the end of the war in Europe. Allied troops reach the Rhine.
  **April**  The resistance launches an attack on Buchenwald's SS. American forces liberate Buchenwald and Dachau. Elie falls

ill with food poisoning. Hitler and Eva Braun commit suicide
in a Berlin bunker.

**May**  General Jodl signs Germany's surrender to the Allies.

**July–August**  Harry Truman, Winston Churchill, Clement Att-
lee, and Joseph Stalin discuss the denazification of Germany.

- **1946**
  The Nuremberg Trials begin to punish war criminals.

- **1947**
  Elie Wiesel enters the Sorbonne in Paris.

- **1948**
  **May 14**  Israel proclaims itself an independent, sovereign state.

- **1952**
  Anne Frank's *Diary of a Young Girl* is published in English.

- **1955**
  François Mauriac convinces Elie to write about the Holocaust.

- **1956**
  Elie Wiesel comes to the United States.

- **1960**
  *Night* is published in English; it originally appeared in 1958, in
  French, as *La Nuit*.

# CRITICAL COMMENTARIES

## FOREWORD

Before a poignant face-to-face visit with a young interviewer for
a Tel Aviv newspaper, French writer François Mauriac describes his
apprehension. After Elie Wiesel knocks at his door, however, he
feels an immediate kinship and tells young Wiesel about the trauma
he suffered when he learned from his wife about Hitler's cruelty
toward children. She had seen trainloads of them at the Austerlitz
station and, at that time, neither Mauriac nor his wife knew about
the death camps. All they knew was that these thousands of children had been separated from their parents.

Wiesel says that he is a death camp survivor, and Mauriac is
deeply moved. He tells us that Wiesel is "one of God's elect." The

elderly Frenchman realizes that the horrors of smoking crematories and their hopeless victims have incarcerated Elie in a perpetual isolation and angst that did not end with the liberation of 1945. Mauriac searches for proof that God is love, but has no evidence to counter Elie's grim testimony. He remembers weeping wordlessly and embracing the young journalist.

## Commentary

Novelist and playwright François Mauriac (1885–1970), one of France's most prestigious Christian writers, was seventy when he met twenty-seven-year-old Elie Wiesel. In the Foreword to *Night*, the first-person documentary that he helped Wiesel publish, Mauriac alludes to the eighteenth-century Enlightenment, an optimistic, progressive period of rational thought from which evolved an overthrow of the monarchy during the French Revolution in 1789. Although he believes in the principles of the Enlightenment and in human advancement, a looming sense of the world's regression into barbarism struck him at the beginning of World War I. Mauriac's pessimism didn't reach its height, however, until the Nazi perversion of science produced efficient death camps as a means of ridding Adolf Hitler's dream state of all people whom he deemed unfit to live in it or to contribute to the building of a Master Race. Mauriac's conclusion forms the central theme in the book: Hitler's annihilation of defenseless children constitutes "absolute evil," an act of heinous destruction with no redeeming purpose.

Mauriac's intense relationship with the young eyewitness leads him to hope that as many people will read Wiesel's *Night* as read Anne Frank's *Diary of a Young Girl*. The two works deal with the same historical era and are written from a Jewish point of view. However, a diversity of setting and action sets them apart.

• Anne Frank's journal describes the day-to-day preparations for a Jewish family's concealment from the SS in the annex of a Dutch import warehouse, where they listen to forbidden radio broadcasts and cheer on the Allies as World War II winds to a close. The diary stops short of the family's arrest, separation, and deportation to a concentration camp, where Anne dies of typhus within months of the war's end.

• A more chilling first-person narration, Elie Wiesel's *Night* introduces a similar trusting attitude that the war will soon end and leave them unscathed. The terrible irony of Elie's deportation with fellow Romanian villagers and his failed attempt to keep his father alive surpasses *The Diary of a Young Girl* in the enormity of SS cruelty, racism, and murderous intent to rid the expanding Third Reich of eleven million human beings whom the Nazis labeled as "undesirables."

Mauriac's pairing of the two eyewitness accounts is a worthy suggestion: any reader captivated by Anne Frank's innocence and stalwart spirit will profit from reading about the collapse of optimism and religious faith revealed in Elie Wiesel's plight. The same irony applies to Wiesel's account: his terror in total isolation and helplessness occurs only months from rescue by Allied forces during the closing weeks of World War II.

---

(Here and in the following sections, difficult words and phrases are explained.)

- **François Mauriac** (frahn **swah** moh ree **ak**)   French Catholic ethicist who assisted the French Resistance by writing anti-Nazi articles. In 1952, Mauriac won the Nobel Prize for literature.

- **the Occupation**   June 22, 1940–October 23, 1944, the period during which Nazis overran France and set up a totalitarian government.

- **Austerlitz** (**ow** stuhr lihtz)   currently Brno, the Czech Republic, in the south-central portion of the country.

- **Nazi** (**naht** see)   shortened form for a member of NSDAP (*Nationalsozialische Deutsche Arbeiterpartei*), the German National Socialist party, which Anton Drexler, Dietrich Eckart, Karl Harrer, and Adolf Hitler inaugurated in 1920 as a racist, totalitarian oppressor of human rights. The shortened form of the party's title remained in use from 1930–1945 as a pejorative expressing the world's distaste for Hitler's thugs.

- **Sighet** (sih **geht**)   a provincial Transylvanian town in the Carpathian Mountains in the far north of Romania near the Russian border, an area which was part of Hungary from 1941–1945, thus contributing to the confusion over Elie Wiesel's nationality. He is alternately identified as Romanian, Hungarian, and Transylvanian.

- **Lazarus** (**la** zuh ruhs)   according to John 11, a biblical character whom Christ raised from the dead. The name is a Romanized variant of Elie's first name, *Eliezer*.

- **Nietzsche** (**nee** chuh)   Friedrich Nietzsche, a late nineteenth-century

German philosopher who proclaimed "God is dead" and proposed the concept of the "superman," an idea that was misappropriated by the Nazis in order to justify their obsession with Aryan superiority.

- **the god of Abraham, of Isaac, of Jacob**   three patriarchs of the book of Genesis. Abraham, son of an idol-maker, was the founder of monotheism in the Western world, the father of Isaac, and the grandfather of Jacob, who later changed his name to Israel and sired its twelve tribes.

- **Rosh Hashanah** (rash hah **shah** nuh)   Hebrew for "New Year," a Jewish holiday observed on the first day of the Jewish month of Tishri (usually in September).

- **that other Jew, his brother**   Jesus, who was born to Jewish parents and reared in the Hebraic tradition, including dedication at the Temple and training in oral disputation with learned men.

- **Zion**   here, the term refers to the Jewish nation; Zionism is a general term applying to the movement to establish a Jewish state in Palestine.

- **Talmud** (**tahl** muhd)   a 45-volume compendium of scriptural interpretation, commentary, and traditions, edited in 500 A.D. and used as a source book of Jewish wisdom to solve problems and settle disputes.

- **cabbala** (kuh **bah** luh)   a philosophy based on mystical interpretations of Judaic prophecy, dreams, visions, wisdom, numerology, scripture, sacred mysteries, and godhood.

- **charnel houses**   mortuaries, or makeshift repositories of the dead.

- **grace**   the Christian concept of a gift that the receiver does not have to deserve; a blessing from God or from a generous donor.

## SEGMENT 1

(**Note:**   Wiesel's book is divided into nine unnumbered segments. It will be easier for you to follow the discussion in these Notes if you number the segments in pencil before you begin reading.)

Near the close of 1941, twelve-year-old Elie Wiesel—son of a devout Romanian shopkeeper and brother to three girls, two older and one younger—recounts his avid pursuit of Hasidic Judaism through study of the Talmud and the cabbala. Lacking a mentor to guide his contemplation of religious mysticism, he turns to Moshe the Beadle, a very poor and pious loner who works as a handyman at the synagogue in Sighet. After other worshippers depart the synagogue following the evening service, Moshe shares private time with Elie. He wisely encourages the impressionable boy to pursue God through questions, but to expect no understanding of God's answers, which remain unsatisfied in the soul until death. Moshe insists that each seeker must rely on inborn traits that will open the way to comprehensible answers suited to the individual.

One day, without warning, Hungarian police arrest Moshe along with other foreigners and take them away aboard cattle cars. Elie weeps for the loss of his tutor. The citizens of Sighet accept exile as a natural burden of war and contend that the deportees are working in Galicia. Months later, Moshe returns to report the fate of the exiles—after they arrived in Poland, they boarded trucks bound for a forest, where they dug huge graves and were systematically machine-gunned. Their killers made sport of tossing babies into the air and using them for targets. After being shot in the leg, Moshe was assumed dead. Traumatized by the slaughter, he weeps as he retells the story. Elie and other villagers conclude that Moshe has lost his mind.

As 1942 and 1943 pass, the people in the village follow the war via London radio news. In the spring of 1944, the success of the Russian front seems to spell doom for the Germans. Knowing Hitler's fierce hatred for Jews, villagers doubt that Hitler can remain in power long enough to kill an entire race. Elie, however, pleads with his father to sell out and immigrate to Palestine; Chlomo insists that he is too old to begin again. News from Budapest warns that fascism is on the rise. Although a villager returns from the capital with accounts of anti-Semitism, optimism continues to prevail. A few days later, German army cars appear on Sighet's streets.

At first, polite German officers take up residence in private homes and live peaceably among Jews. Because synagogues are closed, worshippers pray at the homes of rabbis during Passover week. On the seventh day of the festival, Germans arrest Jewish leaders. Edicts force Jews to remain in their homes for three days and to relinquish gold and other valuables. A decree requires them to identify themselves by wearing a yellow cloth star, symbolic of the Star of David. To fearful Jews, Elie's father makes light of the strictures, particularly the yellow patch proclaiming their Jewishness. More anti-Semitic rules ban Jews from restaurants or cafes, trains, and synagogues. The law confines Jews to their residences after 6 P.M. and forces them to cover their windows and to stoke coal on military trains.

The Germans force Sighet's Jews into two ghettos bounded by barbed wire. The Wiesels live on Serpent Street in the larger settlement in the center of town and make room for relatives whom Germans have turned out of their homes. Optimistic and somewhat smug in their private enclave, the Jews attempt to normalize activities. The Saturday before Pentecost, Stern, a police officer, summons Elie's father to a council meeting. Pale and trembling, Wiesel returns near midnight to announce that they are all to be deported the next day; each person is allowed to take only a few personal items and some food. The president of the Jewish Council knows their destination, but is not allowed to divulge it; rumors declare that they are headed for Hungarian brick factories.

Early Sunday morning, a friendly police inspector knocks at the window to warn the Wiesels of danger. By 4 A.M., families are preparing food for the journey. At 8 A.M., Hungarian police order Jews outside and strike out indiscriminately at old and young with police clubs and rifle butts. Within two hours, all Jews stand in the streets. By 1 P.M., the first convoys begin their march out of Sighet. All day Monday, Elie's exhausted family fasts. On Tuesday, the Wiesels anticipate deportation. To their relief, they are forced to resettle in the small ghetto. Elie leads the way; his father weeps. The small ghetto is littered with possessions that the first deportees abandoned in turmoil. The Wiesels move into Elie's uncle's rooms for four nights. At dawn on Saturday, after a wretched Friday night packed in the synagogue with the remaining Jews, the Wiesels join the last deportees to board railway cattle cars—eighty to a car—and depart.

## Commentary

As often occurs in literature, a speaker may reveal much of self while passing judgment on another character. Significant exposition of the narrator's character evolves from Elie's description of his reliance on Moshe the Beadle, the sole villager who recognizes the impressionable young man's need for guidance. Elie, who is moved by the long history of oppression of the Jews, weeps for the destruction of the Temple of Jerusalem, a historical event that occurred under Nebuchadnezzar after a Jewish revolt in 586 B.C. and a second time in 70 A.D. after Roman troops, led by Titus, quelled a Judaean uprising that had begun four years earlier. According to the chronicle *The Wars of the Jews*:

> While the holy house was on fire, everything was plundered that came to hand, and ten thousand of those that were caught were slain; nor was there a commiseration of any age, or any reverence of gravity. . . . The flame was also carried a long way, and made an echo, together with the groans of those that were slain; and because this hill was high, and the works at the temple were very great, one would have thought that the whole city had been on fire. (V, 1)

This lengthy, detailed account was composed by Josephus, an eyewitness to his people's war against the Romans, who later adopted him as a historian and friend of the Emperor Vespasian.

Still traversing the no man's land of pre-adulthood, Elie defies his father's insistence that cabbala is a study for mature men. During prayers, the boy weeps, but can offer Moshe no reason for his tears. Elie turns to mysticism and the occult as a means of interpreting the bittersweet romanticism of Judaic lore and the Jewish race's fight for survival against waves of anti-Semitism that stain human history from the days of Moses onward. By rereading ten times a single page of the cabbala's medieval interpretation, Elie demonstrates a prodigious drive to come to terms with humanistic concerns. The irony of Elie's immersion in Judaica is his failure to predict another Titus in Adolf Hitler, who retained enough strength in his final days in power to attempt genocide of Europe's Jews.

---

- **beadle**   a minor parish official or caretaker.   / handyman

- **Hasidic** (ha **sih** dihk)   an eighteenth-century group of Jews who stressed the joyous, ecstatic, elements in their faith. The term also describes fiercely orthodox Jews who bind themselves to strict observance of Jewish laws.

- **Transylvania**   a plateau in northwest Romania.

- **cabbala** (kuh **bah** luh)   a medieval system of interpreting scripture by the application of meditation, emotion, mysticism, insight, intuition, communion with God, and numerology.

- **Maimonides** (may **mah** nih deez)   Moses ben Maimon (1135–1204), a Spanish physician and philosopher who fled Muslim persecution by moving his family from Cordoba to Israel, then to Egypt, where he rose to the rank of royal physician. He codified Jewish law, formulated a Jewish creed, wrote scriptural commentary, and compiled a religious guide book.

- **Zohar** (zoh **hahr**)  literally, the "Book of Brightness," a symbolic or allegorical interpretation of Jewish law. Moses de Leon compiled the Zohar, the main text of the cabbala, in Spain near the end of the thirteenth century.

- **Hungarian police**  After Germany forced Romania to cede Transylvania to Hungary on August 30, 1940, the Hungarian police ruled millions of Romanians and, under compulsion of the SS, launched anti-Semitic terrorism against Jews.

- **Galicia, near Kolomaye**  a Slavic territory in the northern Carpathian Mountains which lies partly in Poland and the Ukraine. Kolomaye (modern Kolomyya) is north of Sighet in Russia.

- **Gestapo** (gee **stahp** oh)  the *Geheime Staatspolizei*, or secret state police, an arm of the *Schutzstaffel*, called the SS or Black Shirts, a hand-picked corps of 50,000 secret police who functioned as security officers and as Hitler's body guard. For their fanaticism and devotion to Hitler's dictates, the Gestapo became the most hated and feared of German terrorists.

- **London radio**  After the Nazi takeover of much of Europe, people depended on the BBC (British Broadcasting Company), a state-owned communication system that kept listeners informed of developments in the war.

- **Zionism**  an international drive or political movement that resulted in the development and establishment of a Jewish state.

- **Fascist party**  a political party supporting brutally oppressive, dictatorial control of public speech and civil rights and enforcing uncompromising adherence to inhumane laws. There were German Fascists under Hitler and Italian Fascists under Mussolini.

- **Horthy**  Nikolaus Horthy de Nagybanya, ruler of Hungary, supported Hitler's invasion of Yugoslavia and Russia. In October 1944, he realized that Germany intended to overrun Hungary and defied Hitler. The SS placed him under house arrest in Bavaria, from which American troops released him in 1945.

- **Nyilas**  Hungary's fascist party.

- **the yellow star**  a palm-sized patch centered with a hexagram, the yellow Mogen David, or Magen David, called the Shield of David, or the

Star of David, a regular six-pointed shape composed of two triangles superimposed—one point up and the other point down. Today, the same figure adorns the flag of Israel.

- **Passover** a Jewish holiday that commemorates the departure of Jews from slavery in Egypt under the leadership of Moses, who defied Pharoah following an onslaught of seven plagues that concluded in the death of the firstborn in each household. The Jews avoided the Angel of Death by daubing their doorposts with the blood of a sacrifical lamb.

- **ghetto** a section of a city into which an ethnic or religious minority, lepers, or outcasts are restricted. Jews were required to live in ghettos from medieval times unto the French revolution of 1789, which ended this oppressive practice.

- **Pentecost** a Jewish harvest festival, called *Sukkot* in Hebrew.

- **phylacteries** (fuh **lak** tuh reez) a set of leather cubes containing parchment slips inscribed with biblical passages and bound to the head and left forearm or middle finger during ritual weekday prayers. Phylacteries, also known as tefillin, are a sign of orthodox devotion to Deuteronomy 9:18, a scriptural passage that requires an outward demonstration of piety.

- **captivity of Babylon** In 586 B. C., Nebuchadnezzar put down a Jewish revolt and placed the most prominent Jews in captivity in Babylon, leaving behind the poorest and least troublesome. Although Cyrus of Persia freed the captives in 516 B. C., most chose to remain in their new homeland.

- **Spanish Inquisition** Founded in 1478 by Ferdinand V and Isabella, under Father Tomás de Torquemada, it began torturing "new Christians," Jews who had converted to Christianity but were suspected of having lapsed back into an observance of Judaism, in order to eradicate blasphemy, immorality, infanticide, and homosexuality and to assure that the souls of all of the "heretics" would enter heaven after death. Some suspects were strangled or burned at the stake in public ceremonies; others fled to Turkey. The church enriched itself by confiscating their property.

- **boches** (**bohsh** uz) a derogatory name for Germans. The word is a shortened form of *caboche*, or hardhead.

## SEGMENT 2

For three days these eighty Jews of Sighet travel northwest standing up in hot, wretched, cramped quarters. They crave water and space to lie down; food runs low. At a stop at Kaschau, they realize that the train has entered Czechoslovakia. Germans claim control of the convoy and demand that deportees turn over any valuables or be shot. A similar fate awaits the entire carload if anyone escapes. Their attempts at rest are destroyed by the insane shrieks of Madame Schächter, who is torn by terrifying visions of burning. The others tie her in restraints, force a gag into her mouth, and beat her to control the hysteria.

On the third afternoon, the train halts at the depot of Auschwitz, Poland. Two deportees fetch water and return with false information: families will remain together; the young will work in factories; the elderly and invalids will work in the fields. A German officer promises medical care in the hospital car. Near midnight, the prisoners see flames leaping from a tall chimney. At Birkenau, the reception center for the Auschwitz compound, where the air, rent with flames, smells of incinerated flesh, attendants in striped uniforms, carrying police clubs force everyone out of the railway boxcar.

## Commentary

Elie Wiesel's recollection of Madame Schächter's compelling visions punctuates the text with a fearful, dramatic foreshadowing. Although information gained from various sources provides no proof that a burning furnace of fire awaits them at their destination, the wretched, babbling testimony of a single madwoman rattles the defenseless carload of deportees with her spasmodic clairvoyance fraught with shrieks and pleas for help. Up to this point in the documentary, the Wiesels have discounted Moshe the Beadle's eyewitness accounts of Nazi machine-gun executions and have ignored the knowledgeable police inspector's tap at the covered window. Wiesel implies that the opportunity to immigrate to Palestine and the offer of a refuge with the housekeeper Maria are missed reprieves for his imperiled family, even temporarily, from German state police intent on Jewish extinction.

In later decades, Jews have wrestled with accusations that millions of their forebears complied docilely and meekly accepted confiscation of property, forced labor, torture, medical experimentation, and death. Other evidence, including Wiesel's commentary, proves that counter-insurgents engaged in sabotage, organized a bold network of defiance and disobedience through doctors and

Kapos, and seized control of camps as Allied liberators fought within earshot of dismayed SS staff, who fled in fear of retaliation from the inmates they had whipped, starved, threatened, and demoralized. One of the strongest testimonies to Jewish cunning is Thomas Keneally's *Schindler's List*, a novel filmed in 1993 by Steven Spielberg to honor a Gentile entrepreneur's assistance of 1,100 courageous Jewish workers, especially Itzhak Stern, the Polish Jewish accountant who made out the list of workers whom Oskar Schindler protected with phony work papers, bribes to the SS, and demands for employment. Other rescuers who disprove blame cast on Jews include these:

- a half million members of the French Resistance, of whom 49,000 died or were executed and 200,000 were deported to concentration camps
- Raoul Wallenberg, a Swedish diplomat and exporter who falsified papers for 100,000 Jewish emigres
- King Christian X of Denmark, who donned the yellow star to demonstrate sympathy for Jews and led the Danes in evacuating streams of Jewish refugees to safety

---

- **Auschwitz** (**owsh** vihtz)   the death camp complex built in May 1940, south of the Vistula River a mile from the town of Oswiecim, Poland. Auschwitz I, the original concentration camp, annihilated two million victims with Zyklon B, a hydrocyanic vapor spread through shower heads on unsuspecting victims, then disposed of their remains in crematories. Added to the original buildings was Birkenau, or Auschwitz II, a selection and disposal center at the Auschwitz depot, and the Monowitz labor camp, or Auschwitz III, which lay south of the I. G. Farben synthetic oil and rubber factory, called Buna.

## SEGMENT 3

Past SS guards armed with tommy guns, Elie disembarks and follows the men's line to the left; the women pass to the right. He never sees his mother or sister Tzipora again. A friendly insider advises fourteen-year-old Elie to claim to be eighteen and tells his father to subtract a decade from his fifty years. A cynical voice curses the stupidity of Jews who aren't aware that Auschwitz is a death camp where they will be "burned. Frizzled away. Turned into ashes." A flicker of revolt enlivens a few sturdy men; calming voices urge all to rely on faith. Dr. Mengele, an SS officer, surveys the men, sending the unfit to the crematory, which belches foul smoke and flames into the black sky. Elie claims to be a young farmer. He and his father follow the healthy men to work details. A truck delivers a load of babies, which are tossed into a fiery pit. Elie considers throwing himself into the electric wire rather than be burned with the infants.

Elie's father realizes that no external agency will rescue them. Weeping, he prays, but Elie rebels against his silent god. As they stay together and march past the pit to their barracks, Elie loses his opportunity to kill himself. Vicious trustees force them to strip for another selection. The strongest inmates become crematory workers. Elie remains with his father as the barber shaves their heads. The Wiesels greet friends. Elie lapses into a meditation on self-preservation. Forced into the cold night to another barracks, they disinfect their bodies, then shower. At a third barracks, attendants toss them badly fitting prison clothes, which they exchange among themselves for a better fit.

At the so-called gypsies' camp, Elie and his father enter a mud-floored barracks. A Kapo demands new shoes from anybody who has them; Elie's new shoes are concealed in mud and escape notice. An SS officer warns them that inmates must work or go to the crematory. Separated from skilled locksmiths, electricians, and watchmakers, Elie and Chlomo leave Birkenau and move toward a stone barracks. After a half-hour march through electric fencing they arrive at another camp in Auschwitz, Block 17, where SS officers menace them with machine guns, revolvers, and dogs. Through a shower and into late-night air, they approach garden plots and a smiling, compassionate young Polish prisoner-overseer who alleviates their terror with the first humane words Elie has heard in a long time: "Good night."

After a night's sleep, the new prisoners receive clothes and black coffee. Elie, comparing this place to Birkenau, says that Auschwitz seems like a rest home, after all; he's able to drowse in the spring sun. That afternoon, however, veterans tattoo him with the number A-7713. At roll call, bands play martial music as officers log in returning workers by number. The days pass in a routine of work, food, roll call, bed. Elie reunites with a relative—Stein of Antwerp, who worries about his wife and little sons. At the end of

**Eastern Europe 1944**

Elie Wiesel was born in 1928 in the small village of Sighet in the Carpathian Mountains. In May 1944, Germans forced all Sighet Jews into railway cattle cars. Destination: unknown.

The first stop was Kaschau, Czechoslovakia. A few days later, they arrived at the death camp of Auschwitz. Birkenau was the selection and disposal center; Elie and his father survived the physical selection process and were marched to Buna.

In January 1945, the nearness of the liberating Russian army caused the Buna guards to force all inmates outside, where they were driven through heavy snow to Gleiwitz. Those who survived were loaded into roofless cattle cars for a freezing ten-day journey to Buchenwald. Elie's father died shortly afterward. When the camp was liberated on April 10, Elie could scarcely recognize himself in the mirror: it was the face of a cadaver that stared back at him.

# *Night* Genealogy

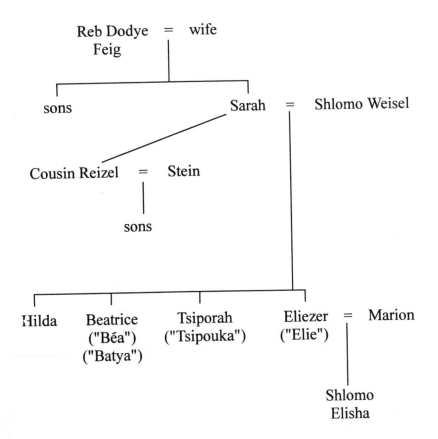

three weeks, the authorities replace the too-humane Polish overseer with a savage man assisted by "real monsters." Not long afterward, the one hundred ordinary workers are ordered out of the block and, after marching through Germans streets, past flirting German girls, they reach a new camp: Buna. An iron gate closes behind them.

## Commentary

Central to the characterization of Elie is the rapid transformation of his personality from a loving, concerned son to a dispassionate survivor. After the gypsy-prisoner Kapo beats Elie's father to the ground for asking permission to go to the toilet, Elie is surprised at himself: he is incapable of making a move and saying anything in his father's defense. The reduction of his humanity to a selfish will to live creates remorse, a significant part of the dehumanization of internees, who learn to preserve their lives at any cost—even in the face of pain and humiliation inflicted on a parent. Still the tender-hearted boy who once wept while praying, Elie judges himself harshly: "Had I changed so much, then? So quickly?" Moving beyond feeling and sleeplessness to an unknown destination, he passes emblems of death's heads that warn internees not to touch the electric fence. The skull precipitates black humor: he says of the mocking placard: "Was there a single place here where you were not in danger of death?"

On the eighth day of prison life, Elie redeems his harsh self-castigation in a minor episode—the spur-of-the-moment lie he tells Stein of Antwerp, the husband of Mrs. Wiesel's niece Reizel. By extending a scrap of hope to Stein that Reizel and the little boys thrive in Antwerp and that they send regular letters to his mother, Elie temporarily relieves Stein's tension, which had begun two years earlier with his deportation. This stroke of grace suggests that Elie, still months from his fifteenth birthday, has acquired some of the maturity and compassion of his father and is capable of lifting himself out of apprehension and grief to bestow hope on a fellow sufferer. This quality in the narrator became a major factor in his receipt of the Nobel Prize, which hundreds of letter-writers supported with testimonials to his selfless character, generosity, and empathy for strangers whom fate had turned into victims.

---

- **tommy gun**   slang name for the Thompson machine gun, a .45-caliber submachine gun invented by John Taliaferro Thompson in the 1920s and issued by the FBI as a standard weapon.

- **Kaddish**  a 2,000-year-old Aramaic prayer, or doxology, recited at funerals, memorial services, and anniversaries of deaths. The prayer, which requires at least ten participants for its recital, says nothing of grief, but looks ahead to a time when God will redeem humankind. It reads:

    Let the glory of God be extolled, let his great name be hallowed, in the world whose creation he willed. May his kingdom soon prevail, in our own day, our own lives, and the life of all Israel, and let us say: Amen.

    Let his great name be blessed for ever and ever. Let the name of the Holy One, blessed is he, be glorified, exalted and honored, though he is beyond all praises, songs and adorations we can utter, and let us say: Amen.

    For us and for all Israel, may the blessing of peace and the promise of life come true. And let us say: Amen.

    May he who causes peace reign in the high heavens. Let peace descend on us, on all Israel, and all the world, and let us say: Amen.

    —Stern, Chaim, ed. *Gates of Prayer.* New York: Central Conference of American Rabbis, 1989.

- *Yitgadal veyitkadach shmé raba*  Hebrew for "May His Name be blessed and magnified."

- *Los!*  German for "Hurry up!" or "Do it now!"

- *Sonder-Kommando*  German for "special command," Jews assigned to remove gassed corpses. They had to remove gold teeth and drag the bodies to carts which transported the dead to the crematorium to be burned. The Nazis promised the *Sonder-Kommando* their lives but this was a deception. Eventually, the *Sonder-Kommando* were themselves gassed.

- **Kapo** (**kah** poh)  German term for trustees or guards chosen from the prisoners themselves. The kapos often preserved their special status by being more cruel than the SS officers.

- **lavatory**  a toilet.

## SEGMENT 4

At Buna, the new camp, which is virtually deserted, Elie and his father undergo the usual shower, new clothes, and waiting period; then they wait in a tent. Their overseer seems humane. Veterans warn them to avoid the building unit. Following a three-day quarantine, three doctors examine the hundred inmates. One of the doctors searches for gold teeth. A band composed of congenial Jewish musicians plays a march as prisoners trudge to the warehouse to work. Elie enjoys Hebrew chants and songs with other Zionist youth and discusses immigration to Haifa.

Despair reigns as savagery becomes more prevalent. The camp dentist demands Elie's gold crown; he saves it by pretending to have a fever. Without warning one day in the warehouse, Idek falls into a murderous fit and lashes Elie, who restrains himself and remains silent. A French Jewess who passes as an Aryan soothes his bloody face. (Years later, he encounters her in the Paris subway and spends an evening reminiscing about their brief friendship and experiences at Buna.) Franek, the foreman, torments Chlomo for marching out of step as a means of preying on Elie's feelings for his father's suffering and thereby extorting the gold tooth. In desperation at his father's torment, Elie allows a dentist from Warsaw to extract his gold crown with a rusty spoon. On a Sunday, Elie angers Idek by laughing after seeing him with a naked Polish girl in a room adjacent to the warehouse. For this indiscretion, Elie is forced to lie on a box and receive twenty-five strokes. He faints and is forced into consciousness to promise to keep Idek's dirty secret.

On another Sunday at 10 A. M., block leaders secure prisoners as air-raid sirens wail. Elie remains unafraid as American planes bomb Buna for over an hour. The prisoners rally, even though they have to remove an unexploded bomb from the prison yard and clear away debris of damaged buildings. A week later, Elie and his fellow workers witness a pre-breakfast hanging of a young man from Warsaw who stole during the alert. Later, in retaliation for the sabotage of the camp power station, the SS torture a Dutch Oberkapo and hang three more people, including a small, angelic-looking thirteen-year-old. Elie is incensed by the fact that the boy is so undersized that he takes over half an hour to die of strangulation. A prisoner demands to know where God is; to himself, Elie replies, "He is hanging here on this gallows."

## Commentary

The spare, almost skeletal quality of Elie Wiesel's prose parallels the depletion of the body, which overrules other needs and thoughts in a constant demand for nourishment. He recalls, "I was a body. Perhaps less than that even: a starved stomach. The stomach alone was aware of the passage of time." In flashes of memory as keen and fleeting as strobe-lit tableaus, the book depicts a few handholds of optimism for young Wiesel: friendly Jews playing in the orchestra, dreams of a free Jewish state in Israel, a secretive Jewess working in the warehouse whom Wiesel later recognizes in the Paris Metro. The fragility of his upbeat mood falls victim to Franek, who demands the gold crown from Elie's mouth. Waves of brutality sweep over earlier moments of camaraderie and swamp the respites of friendship and work with constant fear of beatings and victimization, which fall as haphazardly on the innocent as foretold in the biblical "rain on the just" that Christ cites in the Sermon on the Mount (Matthew 5:45). Wiesel's skillful style pares to a thin, lethal edge the collective hellishness of Buna and his own precarious hold on life. Tearing at his sanity is the fear that his compassion will capsize, leaving him to drown in his animal nature, sacrificing principles and even devotion to his father for the sake of survival.

---

- **Beethoven**   Ludwig von Beethoven, a native of Bonn, Germany, produced dramatic romantic music for piano, strings, orchestra, and ballet. Because of the immediacy and emotional intensity of his works, Nazi laws ban Jewish instrumentalists from playing Beethoven's music. Even more identifiable with the myth of the "master race" were the works of Wagner, which devout Jews are still reluctant to perform.

- *meister* (**my** stuhr)   German for "master."

- **Haifa** (**hy** fuh)   the major port and rail center of Israel. Haifa lies sixty-five miles north of Tel Aviv.

- **Aryan** (**ayr** ee uhn)   Hitler believed that there was an Aryan race, which included Germans—and all other races, including the Jews, were inferior. According to Hitler, "Aryans" were statuesque, blond, and blue-eyed. Ironically, Hitler had none of these traits. In addition, he was wrong about the word "Aryan." The word refers to a group of languages. There is no such thing as an Aryan race. Race, in the nineteenth century, was used in all sorts of contexts. Yet it was linked, so the argument went, with one's "blood," something we would call genetics today. Hitler picked up on this misunderstanding and argued that there was something intrinsically inferior in the Jews' blood which rendered their whole person inferior. Hitler's ideas were wrong. How could the Nazis have called the Jews a race when people of all kinds can *convert* to Judaism. Jews are members of both a religious and an ethnic group—not a race.

- **Metro (may** troh)   the Paris subway system.

- **Himmler**   head of the SS. An ambitious power-monger, Heinrich Himmler served as *Reichsführer*, or second in command, to Hitler and expanded the secret police into a fearful network. The "final solution," or total annihilation of all Jews, was Himmler's prime task. Ousted by Martin Bormann in April 1945, he poisoned himself May 23, 1945.

- **Lagerkapo (lah** guhr **kah** poh)   German for "head of camp."

- *pipel* (**pee** p'l)   German for a "young apprentice" or "assistant."

- **Oberkapo (oh** buhr **kah** poh)   German for "overseer."

## SEGMENT 5

Religious fervor is strong in the fall during celebration of Rosh Hashanah, a holy day marking the beginning of the Jewish year (usually in September). At the camp, 10,000 Jews leave their meal and gather to pray. As the chant of the officiant rises, Elie can only accuse God of forsaking the prisoners, for allowing the crematories to operate. Alienation descends so relentlessly that Elie feels himself turned to ash. On return to his father, Elie kisses his hand and, in silence, experiences a deep sense of unity and understanding. During the celebration of Yom Kippur, Elie obeys his father and does not fast. He interprets the act as a defiance of God. In the former devout heart lies emptiness.

An apprehensive shiver unsettles the camp as the SS begin the selection process to separate the strong from the weak. Only older veterans can laugh and recall harsher times when Kapos filled a quota of rejects each day. Elie has transferred to a building unit and daily drags heavy blocks of stone, while fearing for his father, who is rapidly aging. Following Tibi and Yossi, Elie runs past Dr. Mengele to demonstrate his strength and healthy resilience. Days after the selection, the *Blockaelteste*, the leader of the block, calls Elie's father and nine others from Block 36 for a second examination. Fearful that he will never see Elie again, Chlomo bequeaths his son a knife and spoon, a pitiful inheritance. At the end of the workday, the old man jubilantly reclaims his belongings. Enfeebled by camp life, Akiba loses hope because he realizes that he cannot pass selection and requests that his friends recite the Kaddish in his memory.

Three days later, work and punishment become so insufferable that Akiba's friends forget their promise.

In winter, authorities provide warmer clothes, but work conditions and night temperatures torment inmates. In the middle of January 1945, Elie enters the hospital to undergo surgery to drain pus from the sole of his right foot. A Hungarian Jew warns Elie to leave the ward before the sickest patients are selected for death. To Elie's apprehensive questions, the kindly Jewish surgeon promises that Elie will recover in two weeks. Two days after the surgery, rumors and the sound of guns indicate that the Red Army is approaching. The next day, the SS evacuate inmates to central Germany. Hindered by swelling that won't fit into his shoe, Elie consults with his father. They trudge through snow toward an unknown destination. They later learn that the Russians freed prisoners who remained in the infirmary.

## Commentary

The climax of Wiesel's memoir arrives in his fifteenth year, a time when he begins to view life from a mature perspective. He describes overwhelming emotional turmoil and the illusion of power over God during the prayers of the devout on the eve of Rosh Hashanah. The pace of the prose quickens into a bitter diatribe, an accusation of a deity who allows six crematories to devour Jews day and night, Sundays and feast days. Wiesel permeates his outburst with rhetorical questions:

> Why, but why should I bless Him? . . . How could I say to Him: "Blessed art Thou, Eternal, Master of the Universe, Who chose us from among the races to be tortured day and night, to see our fathers, our mothers, our brothers, end in the crematory?"

The ascending note of anguish presses Elie further into blasphemy and further from the naive young cabbalist who defied his father and sought out the Beadle as a mentor to guide him in the study of the deepest of humanistic questions. As Moshe the Beadle warned, the answers lie in the soul, but remain uninterpreted by the frail mind of man, especially one encumbered with a child's expectation of justice. The age-old quest for an explanation of suffering threatens to subsume Elie, heart and soul.

The dilemma that follows in mid-January grates on the author, who blames himself for choosing to join evacuees to an undisclosed destination rather than to remain in the infirmary and petition the doctor to allow his father to pose as patient or nurse. The sound of gunfire in the distance impedes the internees' sleep the last night at Buna. Elie's decision derives from his distrust of the SS, who may kill all in a final gesture of faith in Hitler's intended annihilation of Jews. The courage to walk through the snowy night on a crudely bound and bleeding foot demonstrates Elie's strong survival instinct. Offsetting his human strength is the brutal weather, which symbolizes the relentless force of nature that has as little mercy on prisoners as Hitler and the SS. Again, there is "rain on the just and the unjust."

---

- **Rosh Hashanah** (rahsh hah **shah** nuh)  a holy day, the first day of the Jewish New Year, a solemn occasion marked by ten days of deep soul searching and repentance.

- **Yom Kippur** (yahm kih **poor**)  the Jewish day of atonement, a holiday observed with fasting and prayer.

- *musulman* (**muh** suhl m'n)  Arabic for "one who surrenders." A synonym for Muslim or follower of Mohammedanism or Islam, the word becomes a prison term for a weak, despondent internee whom the selection committee is certain to relegate to the crematory.

- **Achtung!** (ach **toong**)  German for "Attention!"

- *Stubenaelteste* (**shtyoo** buh nyl **tehs** tuh)  German for "room official."

- *Blockaelteste* (**blah** kyl **tehs** tuh)  German for "block official."

- **Calvary**  a hill in Jerusalem where Christ was crucified. Metaphorically, the term applies to any torture, ordeal, or test of faith.

- **mountebanks**  a phony, or fraud.

- **dysentery** (**dihs** ihn **teh** ree)  a life-threatening intestinal disease causing internal hemorrhaging, diarrhea, and vomiting that dehydrates as it depletes the body of electrolytes.

## SEGMENT 6

Like robots, the prisoners run. The SS shoot all prisoners who fall behind. Elie almost welcomes death as pain and cold impede his flight. Only concern for his father keeps him going through a deserted village and on to a rest stop an hour after dark gives place to light. Elie's father urges him out of the snow and into a ruined brick factory and keeps him awake to save him from freezing. Men lie trampled or freeze to death under a blanket of snow. The kindly old Rabbi Eliahou searches the factory for his son. Elie conceals the fact that the son tried to save himself by outrunning his stumbling parent. Disturbed by the son's disloyalty, Elie prays that he will never abandon his own father.

Even the SS seem weary of the endless flight through snow. On arrival at Gleiwitz, Kapos assign inmates to barracks. Heaps of prisoners nearly crush Elie, who claws and bites his way to a breath of air. In the struggling horde, he hears his friend Juliek, who has brought his violin from Buna. In the dark shed, Juliek produces a fragment of a Beethoven concerto. By morning, Juliek lies dead beside his trampled violin. For three days, closely guarded inmates receive no food or water; outside, the sounds of gunfire revive hopes of the Red Army's advance.

At dawn on the third day, Elie rushes to retrieve his father from an SS selection. The resulting disorder blends survivors with victims. Once more, Elie rescues Chlomo. The inmates march to the rail lines and stand to eat their ration of bread. The SS guards are amused when the prisoners begin scooping snow from each other's backs to quench their thirst. Late that evening, the inmates are still standing when a train of roofless cattle wagons arrives. The SS press a hundred men into each car, and the convoy sets out.

### Commentary

The long, inhumane flight on foot from Buna takes on a surreal quality as death seems preferable to ever-more torment. Elie recognizes death as a wrapping that sticks to his body, a palpable presence that fascinates him, luring him into an insensate state, "Not to feel anything, neither weariness, nor cold, nor anything." At intervals, he closes his eyes and sees "a whole world passing by, to dream a whole lifetime." In a demented state, he envisions himself a master of nature until the dark admits the light of the morning star. Like a benediction, the appearance of its rays precedes the announcement that they have run forty-two miles. Again plunged into a fight with a numbed body, the narrator depicts the eerie hellishness of the scene: "Not a cry of distress, not a groan, nothing but a mass agony, in silence. No one asked anyone else for help. You died because you had to die. There was no fuss." Among stiffening corpses, Elie begins to identify with the dead.

The unity of father and son, a motif from the first night at Birkenau, suggests the love between Abraham and Isaac in the book of Genesis and creates a hopeful scenario. Each agrees to awaken the other after a brief nap. Elie abandons his welcome of death, a personified enemy that slithers silently, peacefully among the sleepers, killing them effortlessly. Elie jostles his neighbors and awakens Chlomo. The reward for the son's diligence is a spontaneous smile from his father. The beneficence of the expression returns Elie to the persona of the questioning cabbalist. In the purgatory of doubt, he demands to know "From which world did it come?"

Elie experiences an epiphany after he recognizes selfish behavior in Rabbi Eliahou's son, who ran ahead to distance himself from his aged, limping burden of a father. Returned in spite of himself to oneness with the Almighty, Elie feels a prayer rise to God and pleads for strength to shelter his father. A later incident confirms the resilience of the human spirit—Juliek plays strains of Beethoven, a pure and uplifting melody. As welcome as a father's smile, as rejuvenating as the prayer that springs unbidden from a bruised spirit, the sweetness of Juliek's gift, a symbol of all art, is a generous restorative that the violinist readily bestows on fellow sufferers. To a shed of dying men, he glides his bow across the strings to produce a comforting strain, a lullaby to the moribund. In daylight, Elie acknowledges Juliek's "lost hopes, his charred past, his extinguished future."

---

- **the morning star**  the planet Venus, which is visible on the eastern horizon shortly before dawn.

## SEGMENT 7

In the heavy, clotted mass of the living and dead, Elie begins to lose hope of survival. By daylight, he locates his father's slumped form but gets no answer to his call. The train halts in a deserted field for the removal of several hundred corpses. Elie slaps his father awake to save him from the "grave diggers," a euphemism for an unfeeling crew who merely dump cadavers on the ground and abandon them. The prisoners live on snow for ten days of travel through

Germany. A German workman precipitates a stampede by tossing bread to starving men, who fight for scraps. A crowd of Germans repeat the gesture and initiate more deadly scrambles for food. A son named Meir beats his father and snatches a crust from his grasp; both men die as others join in the deadly scuffle for bread.

During an unexplained attack on Elie, his father and Meir Katz drive off a would-be strangler. Despite his strength, Meir Katz falls into despair over the selection of his son for death. Elie's father is unable to revive his spirit. Facing icy winds, the prisoners realize they will die if they don't keep active. An outcry from one inmate elicits a mutual wail throughout the convoy. Meir Katz prefers a bullet to continual misery. On arrival at Buchenwald late at night, out of the hundred prisoners in his train car, only Elie, his father, and ten others survive.

## Commentary

This brief chapter carries the ghoulish atmosphere to extremes as more men sink toward death and are matter-of-factly tossed aside. Wiesel's intensification of the danger of violence, hunger, apathy, and cold blurs the lines between bare survival and death. Widespread disinterest in survival within the ranks of dying inmates parallels the callous games workmen play by tossing bread to starving people. Obviously drawn to the passing convoy of prisoners out of curiosity rather than by pity, German workers appear as indifferent to the plight of Jews as are the SS guards. In his later writings and speeches, Wiesel condemns apathy and indifference as the greatest of sins because stifled compassion precipitated complacency and inaction against the war crimes rampant in Hitler's monstrous Third Reich.

The contrast between Meir Katz's loss of hope and the mob of hungry men clawing for food depicts the near-death bestiality that supplants normal human behavior. To Elie, prisoners become "wild beasts of prey, with animal hatred in their eyes; an extraordinary vitality had seized them, sharpening their teeth and nails." The unbridled savagery versus corpse-like inactivity colors a panorama of action versus inaction. At the separation point that elevates humanity from depravity, Wiesel prefigures Segment 8, the arrival at Buchenwald, the Third Reich's oldest concentration camp and the final challenge to Elie's ebbing strength.

---

- **Aden**  a seaport of Yemen on the Arabian peninsula.

- **Buchenwald**  Germany's model concentration camp, which was built outside Weimar in July 1937 to house homosexuals, political dissidents, Russian prisoners of war, Gypsies, and criminals and to supply armaments factories with twelve-hour shifts of camp laborers, who died at the rate of 6,000 per month. Between January and April 1945, the inmate population more than doubled from 40,000 to 81,000. Fifty thousand died from overwork, starvation, and fatal medical experimentation designed to study patient response to bacteria, burns, and lethal injection. The prison staff earned the world's abhorrence for saving tattooed skins.

## SEGMENT 8

Marching in ranks of five past the crematory chimney, Elie and his father hold hands. Elie anticipates a hot bath; his father, who at first is speechless, protests marching to the showers and collapses among corpses. Elie shouts at the failing old man, who becomes infantile and vulnerable in his acceptance of approaching death. A siren sounds; the camp is darkened. The SS drive Elie to the block, where he passes up cauldrons of soup and sleeps on a tiered bed. At daylight, he realizes that he has abandoned Chlomo. Hours later, Elie finds the old man feverish and begging for coffee. Authorities force Elie to leave the barracks until they are cleaned. Five hours later, he returns to his father and discovers that the guards are withholding food from those who are deathly ill. Elie gives him the remains of his soup.

The old man suffers from dysentery. His mind wanders as his strength rapidly dwindles. Three days later, on the way from a bath, he passes his son without recognizing him. Later, in his bunk, he achieves a burst of energy and whispers the location of gold hidden in the family cellar, then lapses into labored breathing. A surgeon refuses to treat him. Elie begins comparing his own attitude toward the old man with that of Rabbi Eliahou's despicable son.

For a week, Elie wrings his hands and hovers at his father's bunk. Nearby prisoners beat the old man because he soils his bedding. The head of the block advises Elie to think of himself, eat both rations of food, and leave his father to die. Elie secretly agrees, then castigates himself with guilt. Because his father continues to call out to Elie, an SS officer whacks the old man's skull with a billy club.

Elie, too weary to keep watch, goes to sleep in an upper bunk. At dawn on January 29, Elie wakes and discovers that another invalid occupies his father's bunk. He assumes that his father has been taken to the crematory and recalls that his father's final word was "Eliezer." Too weary for tears, Elie realizes that death has liberated him from a doomed, irretrievable burden.

## Commentary

The psychological insight of this chapter confronts the reader with the stubborn selfishness that fuels a weary body. Elie, pushed beyond his ability to cope with hunger, cold, disease, camp routine, and cruelty, loses his powers of concentration and exults in the finality of his father's protracted demise. A stark irony arises from the old man's demand for water and from his calls of "Eliezer," a Hebrew name meaning "God will help." Realism demands that Elie accept the truth that God gives neither aid nor dignity to Buchenwald's victims. In Chlomo's final days, he suffers without comfort, medication, or even safety from brutish fellow inmates. The blame Elie heaps on himself creeps through his mind in insidious fears that his father may have been breathing when he was tossed into the oven and burned to ashes. The ignoble death of a kind humanitarian, deeply loved and revered by the citizens of Sighet, gnaws at Elie, a respectful, dutiful son who regrets that he couldn't answer his father's final summons. In his imagination, the absence of prayers and candles darkens the passage of his father's spirit from Buchenwald to its final rest. On January 29, 1945, energized by release from his father's onerous care, Elie begins to live for himself.

## SEGMENT 9

Overcome by trauma, Elie's grief-laden spirit lies beyond pain. Desensitized to external stimulus, he joins the six hundred inmates of the children's block and lives in suspended animation as the front draws near Buchenwald. Only the thought of food permeates his numbness. Rumors arise that the Germans plan a mass annihilation. On April 5, an organized camp resistance refuses the Germans' orders to assemble; Elie joins others in returning to the block. At the rate of thousands per day, the camp is systematically emptied of inmates. No food is distributed to the twenty thousand remaining deportees for the next five days.

An alert sounds on April 10, when the camp officials plan to discharge 20,000 prisoners and blow up the buildings. The evacuation is postponed. Inmates sustain life by eating grass and discarded potato peelings foraged from the ground. The next morning, the resistance exerts pressure on their captors. The children lie on the ground while gunfire and grenades explode above them. Fleeing SS officers abandon the camp to the rebels. At 6:00 P. M., American tanks arrive at the gates.

The prisoners, distracted from revenge by starvation, relieve their hunger with rations of bread. Some young men venture into Weimar for potatoes, clothes, and sexual comfort with local girls. Three days after liberation, Elie contracts food poisoning. After two weeks of serious illness, he recovers enough to look at himself in the mirror for the first time since he left Sighet. He is unable to forget the cadaverous face that stares back at him.

## Commentary

With the conclusion of hostilities in the taut, tense conclusion to *Night*, the arrival of Allied forces effectively halts the Nazi enslavement of the Jews in this camp. However, the battle to reclaim ravaged spirits, to rehabilitate frail, diseased bodies, and to reunite families looms as large as the war to quell genocide. In terms of body, Elie is free, yet, there is no freedom, no emotional reprieve for the sensitive, spiritual boy who once mourned Jewish martyrs of old and wept at his prayers in Sighet. Clearly bereft of will and lacking the strength to join the resistance, he hovers in a spiritual malaise and awaits whatever comes through the gate.

The final scene departs from earlier glimpses of camp life in the depersonalization of Buchenwald and in Elie's catatonic withdrawal from interest in life and self. The nameless, faceless evacuees from the camp matter little to Elie, who no longer clutches at friends or tends his father; even less do his thoughts center on vengeance. Turned inward by starvation, food poisoning, and a primitive form of emotional battery, he continues to fight for life in its most elemental state. The concluding action shows Elie marshalling enough energy to peer into a mirror to witness what torture and forced labor have done to his physical features and expression. The lifelessness of the eyes haunts him with palpable evidence of his nearness to the brink of death.

# CRITICAL ESSAYS

## WIESEL AND THE CRITICS

In characterizing the focus of his work, Wiesel is perhaps his most dogged critic. Unwilling to laud himself as a touchstone of modern documentary journalism and a prime mover in the establishment of Holocaust lore as a unique wing of twentieth-century literature, he thinks of himself as a modest witness rather than moralist, theologian, or sage. In *One Generation After*, he accounts for his method and purpose: "I write in order to understand as much as to be understood." The most prominent of his early writings—the impressionistic trilogy composed of *Night, Dawn* (1961), and *The Accident* (1962)—reports Third Reich savagery with a controlled passion. Fifteen years after the fall of concentration camps, he battled repeated rejections before publishing in 1960 with Hill & Wang the first English version of the trio, translated by Stella Rodway.

In the canon of war literature, *Night* holds a unique position among works that differentiate between the challenge to the warrior and the sufferings of the noncombatant. A terse, merciless testimonial, the book serves as an austere reflection on war that has been characterized as "pure as a police report." Some analysts view the work as allegory in its depiction of the devastating effect of evil on innocence; critic Lawrence Cunningham labels the work a "thanatography."

Although *Night* earned the author a pro forma advance of only $100 and sold only 1,046 copies its first eighteen months, three and a half decades later, *Night* has achieved the status of a nonfiction classic. Alongside Anne Frank's *Diary of a Young Girl*, Corrie ten Boom's *The Hiding Place*, and Thomas Keneally's *Schindler's List*, Wiesel's memoir forms one of the cornerstones of Holocaust reportage.

In the decade following Wiesel's introduction of a verboten topic, few people—even outraged Jews—clamored to hear his grisly, heart-rending narrative, which he typifies as "the truth of a madman." However, critics began reexamining the contribution of Wiesel's shared memoir and elevated the brief nightmarish narrative to the level of a twentieth-century jeremiad:

- For the work's graphic recall of an imponderably monstrous scenario, critic Robert Alter compares Wiesel to Dante, the visionary author who traverses Hell in his *Inferno*.

- Daniel Stern, reviewing for the *Nation*, proclaims the book "the single most powerful literary relic of the Holocaust."

- Lothar Kahn compares Wiesel to an Old Testament prophet and draws a parallel between Wiesel's restless travels and the ceaseless journey of the mythic Wandering Jew, who is said to live forever in spiritual torment.

- Josephine Knopp pairs Wiesel's questioning of God with the biblical rebellions of Abraham, Moses, and Jeremiah.

Subsequent works by Wiesel maintain his attempt to inspire moral activism and his fear that future generations will forget the lessons of history or turn their backs on preventable horrors.

At the pivotal point in Wiesel's career, he was transformed from a spare, insecure after-dinner speaker to America's Holocaust superstar. Awards continue to pour in from B'nai B'rith, the American Jewish Committee, the State of Israel, Artists and Writers for Peace in the Middle East, the Christopher Foundation, and the International Human Rights Law Group. Foundations have established honorariums for humanitarian Holocaust research and Judaica at the University of Haifa, Bar-Ilan University, and the universities of Denver and Florida.

Out of respect for Wiesel's anguished past and his dedication to human rights issues, literary critics temper reviews with a gentled, but pointed rebuttal. In private, their anonymous sneers ring with the intellectual's cynicism. Against the deluge of popular response, their quarrel with Wiesel's lengthy canon is the repetition of Holocaust themes, especially the guilt that the survivor feels for remaining alive through the whims of fate while more pious or scholarly victims died. Some critics denounce Wiesel's obsession with genocide and his belief that God abandoned Jews, who consider themselves a chosen race:

- In 1987, Lawrence L. Langer of the *Washington Post* commented wryly that Wiesel claimed to be finished with the Holocaust, but "the Holocaust has not yet finished with him." Langer added that the author "returns compulsively to the ruins of the Holocaust world."

- Martin Peretz, editor of *The New Republic*, considers Wiesel a public joke and a misapplication of the dignified Nobel Peace Prize.

- *New York Times* reviewer Edward Grossman has accused Wiesel of pursuing a "forced march from despair to affirmation."

- Irving Howe declares in *The New Republic* that Wiesel is a publicity seeker; Alfred Kazin augments the charge with claims that the famed death camp survivor is both shallow and self-aggrandizing.
- Jeffrey Burke of the *New York Times Book Review* carries denunciation to greater extremes by lambasting Wiesel for redundancy and purple prose. Such strong dissent impels Wiesel to unburden his conscience and to master the same objectivity in memoir that he demands of his newspaper reportage.

## AUTOBIOGRAPHY AND HISTORY

The most personal branch of literature, autobiography consists of diaries, journals, letters, and memoirs. As narratives, autobiographies introduce the reader to intimate thoughts and responses of a single point of view at a precise moment in time. In some instances, the eyewitness' account of notable incidents outweighs the lack of artistry, as is the case with the *Diary* of Samuel Pepys, a faithful, if hackneyed account of daily happenings during three significant events in English history—the return of the English monarchy in 1660, the Great Fire, and the Great Plague. In the modern era, Anne Frank's *Diary of a Young Girl* offers the mature observations of a young Jewish girl in an upstairs annex, hidden from the Nazis who overran Holland during World War II. A similar account comes from Zlata Filipovich, who published an account of the Bosnian civil war in *Zlata's Diary*.

In contrast, *Night*, an unadorned recreation of events central to Elie Wiesel's separation from his parents and sisters, offers the reader a significant commentary on a single family's disappearance into the bloodthirsty jaws of Hitler's monstrous war machine. The inevitability of death and despair produces a paradox: a heart-rendingly pathetic isolation of a young Jew from his relatives and from his belief in God, and a thrilling last-minute rescue of one of America's most beloved humanitarians from multiple onslaughts of sickness, hunger, fatigue, and emotional trauma. The incisive style of *Night* shares much with other notable autobiographies:

- Like Benjamin Franklin's *Autobiography*, Wiesel's work dispenses pragmatism and a belief that young people can and should dedicate themselves to higher concerns than frivolity and self-indulgence.

- *Night* shares with St. Augustine's *Confessions* a firm grasp of spirituality, the sustaining force that guides Elie, even when his conscious mind doubts that a deity can still exist and allow death camps to commit wholesale murder.

- In the same vein as Jeanne Wakatsuki Houston's examination of internment in *Farewell to Manzanar*, Elie Wiesel analyzes the faces and gestures of villagers, family, and friends as they prepare to depart from their Romanian home and accept a government-issue barracks as makeshift housing.

- With parallel qualms to those of Yoko Kawashima Watkins in *So Far from the Bamboo Grove*, young Elie describes the last glimpse of a beloved parent who has generously given his time, resources, and worthy counsel to equip his child for a bitter fate amid stony-hearted oppressors.

- Also, Elie Wiesel echoes James Joyce's coming-of-age frankness, a central factor in the success of *A Portrait of the Artist As a Young Man*, a work that lays bare similarly honest and painful revelations grounded in an immature, untried set of values.

As a reconstruction of the author's ego at a crucial moment in world history, *Night* demonstrates the narrator's willingness to face certain death and to cling to the shreds of sanity that remain. Wiesel's command of details forces the reader to observe vicious dogs, to hear the cries of a befuddled old rabbi, to smell the fear in the fleeing evacuees who race through the night toward an unknown fate, to hear a Beethoven melody pierce the night, and to touch the cold, motionless form of the violinist who has expended the last of his artistry in a musical benediction over a scene of heartless savagery.

### THE FOCUS ON "NIGHT" AS A SYMBOL

The choice of *La Nuit* (Night) as the title of Elie Wiesel's documentary work is propitious in that it epitomizes both physical darkness and the darkness of the soul. Because young Elie and his father observe the sacrifice of a truckload of children in a fiery ditch and watch the flaming corpses light up the night sky at Birkenau, the darkness evokes multiple implications. The crisply methodical work of the Nazi death camps spreads over night and day and actualizes the fanatical intent of Hitler to wipe out all traces of European Jewry. The night that enshrouds their humanity obliterates mercy and human feeling: so long as the perpetrators of consummate evil can view genocide as a worthy job, the "night" of their soullessness shines in medals and commendations for their commitment to the Nazi world view, which pictures a future of blue-eyed blondes, all derived from Gentile backgrounds.

More significant than these intertwined forms of night is the darkening of young Elie's idealism. Once moved to identify with past martyrs of the Babylonian Captivity and the Spanish Inquisition, he finds himself standing outside the romantic episodes of historical anti-Semitism on a dismal scene that his eyes absorb in disbelief. He refrains from wondering if the smoky wreath over Auschwitz's crematories contains the ashes of his mother and sisters. By depersonalizing the fears that lurk in his subconscious and that overwhelm the badly shaken Chlomo, Elie concentrates on food, warmth, and rest. The instinctive need to pray falters on his mind's surface, yet, deep within, he continues to fight the descent of spiritual night that threatens to obliterate God from his being.

On a global scale, Wiesel the writer chooses to incubate the darkness of his memories for a decade, then, at the age of twenty-six, to heed the urgent request of François Mauriac to unveil to the world a front-row memoir of Hitler's hellish night, the palpable blackness that fills his eyes with smoke, his nostrils with the stench of scorched flesh, and his ears with inarticulate cries of the dying. The particularized scenes he flashes on his verbal screen become mere suggestions of a reality that only Holocaust survivors can share. Even though words will always fail his purpose, he persists in recreating his battle against the sooty residue that coats his soul and robs him of his most precious tie with childhood—the orthodox faith that motivated him to pray, read, study, and tread the path of Hasidic Judaism.

In Wiesel's Nobel Prize acceptance speech, he recalled a young man discovering "the kingdom of the night." Like Dante winding downward on a horrific spiral into Hell, young Elie questions how such negation of light can rob the twentieth century of its progress in human relations. At the age of fifty-eight, Elie the Nobelist confronted the reality of the metaphoric night: it is the silence of apathy, the wordlessness of bystanders who knew the truth of Hitler's death camps but who took no action, made no objection. Like the lone crier who alarms the village to fire, theft, or massacres of old, Elie the Nobelist, Elie the cavalier, finds no rest in his battle against the incessant fall of night. Wherever the shroud of inhumanity descends—on prisons, battlefields, or the pathless flight of refugees—he stirs himself to sound the alarm, to bid the world to strike back at an enveloping cynicism that tempts humanity to turn aside and say nothing.

## ELIE WIESEL AND MYSTICISM

Early in his exploration of self, young Elie ignores his father's warning about the cabbala and studies a mystical philosophy that demands a maturity and sophistication that comes only from experience. According to the dictates of Moses Cordovero, the cabbalist is expected to imitate thirteen divine qualities, cultivated through daily prayer:

1. Forbearance of detraction or insult
2. Patience in facing evil
3. Forgiveness of evil
4. Understanding of other human beings
5. Control of anger in thought and deed
6. Mercy toward all, even the persecutor
7. Denial of vengeance
8. Concentration on the good in villains
9. Uncompromising compassion for those in pain
10. Honesty
11. Mercy on people who do good
12. Nonjudgmental reproof of villains
13. Respect for the pure, unblemished self that existed in infancy

The culmination of this mystical regimen is the egoless self, a Jewish parallel of the tao, the path to sublime oneness with God.

## ELIE WIESEL AND EXISTENTIALISM

As did Ernest Hemingway, Albert Camus, and Simone de Beauvoir, Elie Wiesel expresses a relentless inner compunction to interpret twentieth-century events that confuse, frustrate, or dismay. He writes about his role in World War II to better understand the suffering of Hitler's victims. His conclusions present a grim reckoning of anti-Semitism and death camp philosophy. An avid student of existentialism, which he encountered in the late 1940s under the instruction of novelist Jean-Paul Sartre at the Sorbonne, a French university famous for preparing students of the humanities, Wiesel is heir to the European philosophers, theologians, and writers of the 1920s and 1930s who delineate human significance in terms of action. According to the existentialist's code:

1. Human beings are often forced into terror and alienation because of their inability to know the future or to control what is done to them or taken from them.
2. Often political situations create a world vision that is absurd, haphazard, destructive, and vicious toward the hapless individual.
3. People sometimes attempt to escape meaningless suffering, even when the effort causes them more pain, a re-evaluation of life, loss, disillusion, alienation from tradition, or death.
4. In assuring their own survival, people may disappoint, betray, or abandon friends and family.
5. The only source of redemption for the world's cruelty and suffering must come from individuals willing to confront their oppressors.

Existentialism defines the hero as a solitary figure who transcends human weakness to undergo absurdly meaningless peril. Goaded by a need to penetrate the mysteries of the universe, this lone hero must abide by the dictates of conscience and exert finite, human powers to break free from isolation, anguish, passivity, or despair. As demonstrated in *Night*, the redemptive power of commitment, spirituality, moral tenacity, and integrity resides in action—the localized, often feeble performance of forgiveness, charity, and acceptance of others.

## ELIE WIESEL AND THE WANDERING JEW

A familiar figure in European lore is Ahasuerus, a mortal doomed to live forever. His legend, first published in Leiden, the Netherlands, in an anonymous monograph dated 1602, predates the printed version and describes a Jew from Hamburg who had been a contemporary of Jesus Christ, who was crucified around 30 A. D. When Jerusalem's mockers demanded that Jesus was a false claimant of the title of Messiah or savior of the human race, Ahasuerus joined the mob and taunted Jesus on the way to the Crucifixion. In token of the Jew's rejection, Jesus promised that Ahasuerus would remain alive until the Second Coming, when the Messiah would return from heaven to fulfill biblical prophecy.

The haunting story of Ahasuerus spread over Europe and found its way into numerous artistic and literary works—in direct reference and subtle allusion. The eternal wanderer, known in French as *le juif errant*, spawned a body of lore that is the opposite of the Faust legend: instead of avoiding death, the Wandering Jew, the only living witness to Jesus' execution, craves an end to the curse of immortality, which he bears like a cross in his search for a final resting place. The modern critical community draws parallels between the miraculously long-lived Jew and the restless Elie Wiesel, whose journalistic and humanitarian travels keep him perpetually on the road, often for the purpose of drawing to the world's attention an untenable condition that threatens nations with war, famine, starvation, or genocide. The potential for romanticism dims beside the real man, an obviously weary benefactor of humanity who expects neither praise nor remuneration for his crusade. The comparison with the Wandering Jew ennobles Dr. Wiesel, a stalwart witness to the world's most dreadful era of systematic annihilation of an innocent race.

## THE THEME OF FAITH

From the beginning, Elie Wiesel's work details the threshold of his adult awareness of Judaism, its history, and its significance to the devout. His emotional response to stories of past persecution contribute to his faith, which he values as a belief system rich with tradition and unique in its philosophy. A divisive issue between young Elie and Chlomo is the study of supernatural lore, a subset of Judaic wisdom that lies outside the realm of Chlomo's pragmatism. To Chlomo, the good Jew attends services, prays, rears a family according to biblical dictates, celebrates religious festivals, and reaches out to the needy, whatever their faith.

From age twelve onward, Elie deviates from his father's path by remaining in the synagogue after the others leave and conducting with Moshe the Beadle an intense questioning of the truths within a small segment of mystic lore. The emotional gravity of Elie's study unites with the early adolescent penchant for obsession, particularly of a topic as entrancing as the history of the Spanish Inquisition or the Babylonian Captivity. Moshe's mutterings strike a respondent chord in Elie as he ponders prophecy of the Messiah, "such snatches as you could hear told of the suffering of the divinity, of the Exile of Providence, who, according to the cabbala, awaits his deliverance in that of man." It comes as no surprise that Elie's personal test jars his youthful faith with demands and temptations to doubt because he lacks experience with evil.

When Moshe returns from his own testing in the Galician forest, his story seems incredible to Sighet's Jews, including Elie. Later, the test of faith that undermines Elie's belief in a merciful God is the first night at Birkenau and the immolation of infants in a fiery trench. The internal battlefield of Elie's conscience gives him no peace as atrocities become commonplace, including hangings before breakfast. The author's admission of weakness casts no doubt on his uprightness; rather, the back and forth debate that empties the core of faith from his heart proves his sincerity toward God, whom he perpetually reaches toward with fearful hands. The extreme realism of Elie's test of faith at Auschwitz portrays in miniature the widespread question of suffering that afflicts Europe's Jews during an era when no one is safe, and no one can count on tomorrow. Although Elie omits fasting and forgets to say Kaddish for Akiba Drumer, the fact that Elie incubates the book for a decade and writes an original text of 800 pages proves that the explanation of faith and undeserved suffering is a subject that a teenage boy is poorly equipped to tackle.

## THE STATE OF ISRAEL

Since biblical times—but especially since the beginning of the mid-nineteenth century—Jews have longed for a permanent home in the Holy Land, a stretch of rugged, but historically significant land on the eastern Mediterranean shore, stretching north from the Gulf of Aqaba over the Negev Desert, west of the Dead Sea and Jordan, and north to the borders of Syria and Lebanon.

The early name for this area of land was Palestine, first settled by agricultural people around 8000 B.C. Hebrew tribes began populating the land in the twelfth century B.C., and eventually it was ruled by Saul, David, and Solomon around 1000 B.C. The kingdom later split into two states, Israel and Judah, which were, in turn, conquered by the Assyrians and the Babylonians. Afterward, the area was ruled by foreign powers—the Persians, Alexander the Great, and the Ptolemies, among others.

Romans took possession of the country in 63 B.C. and stationed Herod the Great on the throne in 37 B.C. Jesus was born into this Roman-ruled, Jewish world which would, after his crucifixion, become a Christian nation. Some 500 years later, Arabs took possession, and it became an Islamic nation; by the tenth century A.D., most of the inhabitants had converted to Islam. In 1099, Western crusaders established rule, but they were eventually routed by armies of the Egyptian sultans, the Mamelukes. In 1516, the country became part of the mighty Ottoman Empire.

The influx of European Jews into the area began in the mid- to late-nineteenth century. Jews living in Europe, especially those in Poland and Russia, fled from Cossack butchery and Russian pogroms, or massacres, and began immigrating into this part of the Ottoman Empire, where they established primitive farming communities. United by a common religion and the Hebrew language, they were fervent in their belief—despite having to live in crude huts and tents, exposed to the continual menace of malaria, and resented by their unfriendly Palestinian neighbors—that they had returned to a land that had, since biblical times, been divinely promised to them as a national home.

At the beginning of World War I, Great Britain inflamed the passion for a Jewish homeland on an international level by issuing the Balfour Declaration, promising a home for the Jewish people within Palestine. The war ended in 1918 and Great Britain supplanted the crumbling Turkish influence; Palestine was now in the hands of the British. The League of Nations further sanctioned the role of Great Britain in creating a Jewish state.

The plan for a Jewish homeland began to founder as Arabs realized that Zionism had spurred an immense, unprecedented immigration of Jews who suddenly destabilized a centuries-old Arab milieu. The newcomers' land-grabbing, communal living, and insistence on gender equality angered and appalled the native Palestinians, and outbreaks of hostility soon led to bloody confrontations.

Ever greater waves of Jewish immigration to Palestine resulted from the growth of Nazi hate groups in Germany and its fascist satellites during the 1930s. In 1935, for example, over 61,000 European Jews felt so threatened that they left their homes, jobs, and families and immigrated to Palestine. From 1936–39, Palestinians erupted in a series of riots, trying to force Britain out of power to save what they considered their ancestral land from the mounting tide of Zionists.

The world's reaction to the execution of six million Jews during the Holocaust forced the matter of a Jewish homeland onto the agenda of the fledgling United Nations. On November 29, 1947, the U.N. General Assembly approved a partition of lands, dividing Palestine into an Arab state and a Jewish state. On May 13, 1948, British peacekeepers relinquished their control.

The next day, Jewish Zionists proclaimed Israel a sovereign state, with David Ben-Gurion as leader. A day later, Jordanian and Egyptian forces invaded the new nation and initiated a bloody era of terrorism, open warfare, and usurpation. During the first year of the new Jewish state, over 6,000 Jews were killed. By this time, however, Israel was now a militarily strong and victorious nation. It had increased its original territory by fifty percent and had reclaimed Jerusalem, a city held sacred by Jews, Muslims, and Christians.

During the following years, the displacement of Arab refugees after they had lost their lands to Israel in military upheavals kept the area in a perpetual state of unrest, including the war for control of the Suez Canal in 1956, the Six-Day War in 1967 (which increased Israel's territory two hundred percent), the assassination of Israeli athletes at the Olympic Games in 1972, and the Yom Kippur War in 1973.

A respite from continuous war between Israel and its neighbors took place in 1979 at Camp David, Maryland. During a meeting brokered by U.S. president Carter, President Sadat of Egypt met with Israel's Prime Minister Begin, and both men signed the first peace treaty between Israel and one of its Arab neighbors. Israel agreed to return the oil-rich fields of the Sinai to Egypt, and, in return, Egypt, a powerful Arab state, officially recognized Israel as a state. In addition, Israel also agreed to work for peace, including an eventual plan for Palestinian autonomy.

War broke out again in 1982 when PLO guerrillas in southern Lebanon began mounting raids into Israel. In retaliation, Israel bombed Beirut for nearly two months and successfully routed Yasir Arafat and his army from the country.

Eleven years later, in September 1993, despite strained relations, Yasir Arafat, leader of the Palestine Liberation Organization, Israeli prime minister Yitzhak Rabin, and Israeli foreign minister

Shimon Peres signed an accord in Washington, D.C., stating that Israel and the PLO recognized each other's right to exist. The PLO promised to abandon its terroristic holy war against Israel, and Israel, in turn, granted self-rule to the Palestinian entities of the West Bank and the Gaza Strip. Rabin, Peres, and Arafat later shared the 1994 Nobel Peace Prize.

Today's Israel, about the size of Massachusetts, is a highly urbanized nation, peerlessly democratic in its social laws, and in an area of the world where religious wars are commonplace, freedom of religion is guaranteed by law to Muslims and Christians living in the country. In addition, Israel has become one of the world's most envied nations in providing educational and health care services to its people. In terms of its economy, the nation is heavily dependent on oil for its energy, and thus it is a major Mediterranean ally in the U.S. struggle to protect the oil fields that fuel the world's industrial growth of the latter half of the twentieth century.

## LITERARY DEVICES

A professional journalist of Elie Wiesel's experience demonstrates that a knowledge and application of literary devices become a natural part of writing. Sprinkled sparsely, yet precisely through the straightforward narrative are language patterns that enhance thought and emotion. For example:

### exclamations
- Have mercy on him! I, his only son!
- Blessed be the Name of the Eternal!

### periodic sentences
- I would often sit with him in the evening after the service, listening to his stories and trying my hardest to understand his grief.
- Despite the trials and privations, his face still shone with his inner purity.

### balanced sentences
- I had known that he was at the end, on the brink of death, and yet I had abandoned him.
- During the day I studied the Talmud, and at night I ran to the synagogue to weep over the destruction of the Temple.

**extended appositives**
- The Jews of Sighet—that little town in Transylvania where I spent my childhood—were very fond of him.
- Suddenly, someone threw his arms around my neck in an embrace: Yechiel, brother of the rabbi of Sighet.

**sentence fragments**
- Revolvers, machine guns, police dogs.
- Perhaps less than that even: a starved stomach.

**similes**
- He looked us over as if we were a pack of leprous dogs hanging onto our lives.
- Monday passed like a small summer cloud, like a dream in the first daylight hours.

**rhetorical questions**
- Had I changed so much, then?
- Poor Father! Of what then did you die?

**cause and effect**
- "Man raises himself toward God by the questions he asks Him," he was fond of repeating.
- To this day, whenever I hear Beethoven played my eyes close and out of the dark rises the sad, pale face of my Polish friend, as he said farewell on his violin to an audience of dying men.

**dialogue**
- "I can see them, son. I can see them all right. Let them sleep. It's so long since they closed their eyes . . . They are exhausted . . . exhausted . . . "
His voice was tender.
I yelled against the wind:
"They'll never wake again! Never! Don't you understand?"

- "What do you want?"
"My father's ill," I answered for him. "Dysentery . . . "
"Dysentery? That's not my business. I'm a surgeon. Go on! Make room for the others."

**foreshadowing**
- Jews, listen to me! I can see a fire! There are huge flames! It is a furnace.

- The Jews in Budapest are living in an atmosphere of fear and terror. There are anti-Semitic incidents every day, in the streets, in the trains.

**short declarative sentences**
- I hadn't any strength left for running. And my son didn't notice. That's all I know.
- I was fifteen years old.

## A NOTE ON TRANSLATION

Because the Stella Rodway translation of Wiesel's original text transfers thought from French to English, it loses the cadence, line length, rhyme, and lingual stress of the original language, particularly alliteration and onomatopoeia. For example, an extended parallel structure expresses Elie's disillusion in Section 3, a dramatic outpouring which is cited below in French with an interlinear translation:

*Jamais je n'oublierai ces instants qui assassinèrent mon Dieu et*
Never shall I forget those moments which murdered my God and

*mon âme, et mes rêves qui prirent le visage du désert.*
my soul and turned my dreams to dust.

*Jamais je n'oublierai cela, même si j'éstis condamné à vivre aussi*
Never shall I forget these things, even if I am condemned to live as

*longtemps que Dieu lui-même. Jamais.*
long as God Himself. Never.

When translators such as Rodway move from one modern language to another, they recover no more than eighty percent of the connotative, or implied, meaning of the text—particularly one that utilizes German titles as well as bits of Hebrew. An even greater challenge is translation of an ancient text, such as the Bible or the cabbala, into a modern language. The resultant version must leap over centuries of social customs, idioms, and human progress to produce an inkling of the motivation and verbal mastery of the primary author. Thus, translators regularly apply their special skills to ancient texts to maintain a close contact with the intent and meaning of the original writer.

# REVIEW QUESTIONS AND ESSAY TOPICS

(1). Contrast Elie Wiesel's experiences in war with those of the main characters in Thomas Keneally's *Schindler's List*, Pearl Buck's *The Good Earth*, Thomas Berger's *Little Big Man*, Walter Dean Myers' *Fallen Angels*, Jessamyn West's *Except for Me and Thee*, Isabel Allende's *House of the Spirits*, Amy Tan's *Kitchen God's Wife*, Michael Schaara's *Killer Angels*, Laura Esquivel's *Like Water for Chocolate*, Richard Rashke's *Escape from Sobibor*, Art Spiegelman's *Maus: A Survivor's Tale*, or Erich Maria Remarque's *All Quiet on the Western Front*. Contrast the needs, fears, and frustrations of both combatants and noncombatants, particularly children, as you account for atrocities.

(2). Compare young Elie's coping skills to those of the main characters in Anne Frank's *Diary of a Young Girl*, Leon Uris' *Exodus*, Jeanne Wakatsuki Houston and James Houston's *Farewell to Manzanar*, Everett Alvarez' *Chained Eagle*, Esther Hautzig's *The Endless Steppe*, Theodora Kroeber's *Ishi*, Zlata Filipovich in *Zlata's Diary*, Toni Morrison's *Beloved*, Yoko Kawashima Watkins's *So Far from the Bamboo Grove*, John G. Neihardt's *Black Elk Speaks*, or Corrie ten Boom in *The Hiding Place*. Discuss activities that enable inmates to endure hunger, despair, terror, loss, and loneliness. For example, evaluate the importance of music, gossip, gifts, laughter, shared meals or chores, walking together, and keeping watch over loved ones.

(3). Contrast authority figures in terms of their lasting influence on Elie and his persistent and thorough self-study. Consider his father and mother, Moshe the Beadle, Idek, Dr. Mengele, overseers, SS guards, the Jewish doctor and Czechoslovakian dentist, and the Allied soldiers who set him free.

(4). Using *Night* as a model, compose extended definitions of repression, autobiography, realism, first-person narrative, literary foils, protagonist/antagonist, allusion, aphorism, polemics, irony, oral tradition, denouement, dialogue, symbol, rhetorical question, existentialism, documentary, surrealism, and parallelism.

(5). Contrast a child's eye view of World War II as opposed to a journal written by a Kapo, a resistance member, Meir Katz, Stein of Antwerp, Chlomo Wiesel, Madame Schächter, Moshe the Beadle, Rabbi Eliahou, Franek the violinist, the Jewish surgeon, the rapacious Polish dentist, or a member of the Red Army.

(6). Analyze the stratification of camp personnel into children, adult males, adult females, workers, *musulmen*, Kapos, guards, *pipels*, SS troops, and supervisors. Explain why it is useful to the German camp to keep healthy workers alive and productive, then kill them and replace them with fresh inmates after the original crew is too weary or ill to work.

(7). Describe the support system that fellow Jews share, particularly holidays, rituals, and prayers. Discuss the importance of the Kaddish and its meaning when applied to countless victims. How do early scenes of prayer and study of cabbala contrast with Elie's loss of reverence for God and his inability to fast? Why does he neglect to say Kaddish for Akiba Drumer?

(8). Account for the ghetto dwellers' lack of concern for rumors of violence and genocide aimed at Jews. Express Elie's regrets that his family does not accept their housekeeper's offer of a hiding place or immigrate to Palestine.

(9). Analyze relationships between father and son, mother and son, teacher and pupil, and fellow Jews, internees, and workers. Explain why Elie seems alone in his contemplation of pain and evil.

(10). Compare the experiences of workers and freedom fighters in the films *Sophie's Choice, Schindler's List, Shoah, The Holocaust, Exodus, A Town Like Alice, Julia,* and *Playing for Time.* How would a filming of *Night* depict Chlomo and Elie during selection? at their jobs? during the flight of the SS?

(11). Summarize themes of Maimonides' writings that have influenced Elie Wiesel's character and outreach.

(12). Contrast the anti-Nazi sentiments of Israel's Haganah and Mosad, Simon Wiesenthal, Raoul Wallenberg, Corrie ten Boom, Otto Frank, Dietrich Bonhoeffer, Anne Frank, Hannah Arendt, Winston Churchill, Franklin D. Roosevelt, and Edward R. Murrow with those of Elie Wiesel.

(13). Apply the defiance and outrage of Yevgeny Yevtushenko's "Babi Yar" or Donald Davidson's "Lee in the Mountains" to that of *Night*.

(14). Relate to Elie Wiesel's fervent fight against moral apathy the words of Pastor Martin Niemoller concerning Nazi genocide:

> In Germany they first came for the Communists and I didn't speak up because I wasn't a Communist. Then they came for the Jews and I didn't speak up because I wasn't a Jew. Then they came for the trade unionists, and I didn't speak up because I wasn't a trade unionist. Then they came for the Catholics, and I didn't speak up because I was a Protestant. Then they came for me—and by that time no one was left to speak up.

(15). Compare the strengths of the speaker of Lord Byron's *Prisoner of Chillon* with those of Elie Wiesel and other survivors of the death camps. Append a comment on the poignant release of both narrators from captivity.

(16). In his *All Rivers Run to the Sea*, Wiesel comments on the witness' burden: " . . . the truth I present is unvarnished; I cannot do otherwise. 'Sing or die,' said Heine. Write or disappear. . . . For me literature must have an ethical dimension. The aim of the literature I call testimony is to disturb." Why does Wiesel prefer the martyr's stance to the more decorative philosophy of "art for art's sake"? How does his attitude toward "[putting] questions to God" cast him as a perpetual sufferer and doomsayer, a combination of the biblical Job and Jeremiah?

(17). Locate scenes in which the physical, emotional, and moral landscapes fall into contrasting patches of light and dark. Express the meaning of the title as it applies to these scenes.

(18). In his Nobel Prize acceptance speech, Wiesel stressed, "Neutrality helps the oppressor, never the victim." Discuss his concept of activism. Include evidence from his life as a journalist and as spokesman for modern Judaism of his active support of humanism and peace.

(19). Explain how the "phenomen" in Chapter 5 of Chaim Potok's *The Chosen* reflects the development of Elie Wiesel as a scholar and holy man.

## SELECTED BIBLIOGRAPHY

ABRAMSON, IRVING. *Against Silence: The Voice and Vision of Elie Wiesel*. New York: Holocaust Publications, 1985.

_____. "Elie Wiesel: Speaking Truth to Power," *Reform Judaism*, Fall 1985, 27.

ALTER, ROBERT. *After the Tradition*. New York: E. P. Dutton, 1962.

APPLEFIELD, CATHERINE. "A Passover Seder Hosted by Elie Wiesel," *Billboard*, April 29, 1995, 78.

BROWN, ROBERT M. *Elie Wiesel: Messenger to All Humanity*. South Bend, Indiana: University of Notre Dame Press, 1986.

CARGAS, HARRY JAMES, ed. *Conversations with Elie Wiesel*. South Bend, Indiana: Diamond Communications, 1992.

_____. *Responses to Elie Wiesel*. New York: Persea Books, 1978.

_____. *Telling the Tale: A Tribute to Elie Wiesel on the Occasion of His 65th Birthday: Essays, Reflections & Poems*. St. Louis, Missouri: Time Being Books, 1993.

CLINES, FRANCIS X. "Wiesel, Accepting the Nobel, Asks the Living to Remember," *New York Times*, December 11, 1986, 1.

*Contemporary Authors*. CD-ROM. Detroit: Gale, 1994.

*Contemporary Literary Criticism*. Volume 37. Detroit: Gale, 1986.

DAVIS, COLIN. *Elie Wiesel's Secretive Texts.* Gainesville: University Press of Florida, 1994.

DEVEREAUX, ELIZABETH. "A Memoir from Wiesel," *Publishers Weekly,* October 23, 1995, 33.

_____. "Elie Wiesel," *Publisher's Weekly,* April 6, 1992, 39.

*Discovering Authors.* CD-ROM. Detroit: Gale, 1993.

DORFMAN, JONATHAN. "The Paradox of Elie Wiesel," *Boston Globe,* March 13, 1991, 78.

FISKE, EDWARD B. "Elie Wiesel: Archivist with a Mission," *New York Times,* January 31, 1973, 64.

FREEDMAN, SAMUEL G. "Bearing Witness: The Life and Work of Elie Wiesel," *New York Times Magazine,* October 23, 1983.

FRIEDMAN, MAURICE. *You Are My Witness.* New York: Farrar, Straus, and Giroux, 1987.

GREENE, CAROL. *Elie Wiesel: Messenger from the Holocaust.* Chicago: Children's Press, 1987.

KAHN, LOTHAR. *Mirrors of the Jewish Mind.* A. S. Barnes, 1968.

KAKUTANI, MICHIKO. "Rich, Personal Revelations Stir Tide of Emotions," *Charlotte Observer,* December 31, 1995, G5-6.

KAMM, HENRY. "Marchers with Food Aid Get No Cambodian Response," *New York Times,* February 7, 1980, A3.

KIMMELMAN, MICHAEL. "Making Art of the Holocaust: New Museum, New Works," *New York Times,* April 23, 1993, A24.

KNOPP, JOSEPHINE. "Wiesel and the Absurd," *Contemporary Literature,* University of Wisconsin, Spring 1974, 212-220.

LAZO, CAROLINE. *Elie Wiesel.* New York: Macmillan, 1994.

MARKHAM, JAMES M. "Elie Wiesel Gets Nobel Prize for Peace as 'Messenger,'" *New York Times*, October 15, 1986, A10.

PARISER, MICHAEL. *Elie Wiesel: Bearing Witness*. Brookfield, Connecticut: Millbrook, 1994.

PATTERSON, DAVID. *In Dialogue and Dilemma with Elie Wiesel*. Durango, Colorado: Hollowbrook, 1992.

RITTNER, CAROL. *Elie Wiesel: Between Memory and Hope*. New York: New York University Press, 1991.

ROSENFELD, ALVIN H. *Confronting the Holocaust: The Impact of Elie Wiesel*. Ann Arbor: Books on Demand, 1987.

SCHUMAN, MICHAEL A. *Elie Wiesel: Voice from the Holocaust*. Hillside, N. J.: Enslow, 1994.

STERN, DANIEL. "The Word Testifies for the Dead," *Nation*, January 5, 1974, 24–26.

STERN, ELLEN. *Elie Wiesel: Witness to Life*. New York: Ktav Publishing, 1982.

WALKER, GRAHAM B., JR. *Elie Wiesel: A Challenge to Theology*. Jefferson, N. C.: McFarland, 1987.

WIESEL, ELIE. *La Nuit*. Paris: Les Éditions de Minuit, 1958.

ZOGLIN, RICHARD. "Lives of Spirit and Dedication," *Time*, October 27, 1986.

## HISTORICAL BACKGROUND

ADLER, DAVID A. *We Do Remember the Holocaust*. New York: Henry Holt, 1989.

ATKINSON, RICK. "Amid 'Ashes of Souls,' Auschwitz Survivors Gather," *Charlotte Observer*, January 27, 1995, 1A, 8A.

DAWIDOWICZ, LUCY S. *The War Against the Jews, 1933–1945.* New York: Holt, Rinehart and Winston, 1975.

GILBERT, MARTIN. *The Holocaust.* New York: Holt, Rinehart & Winston, 1985.

GUTMAN, YISRAEL, ed. *Encyclopedia of the Holocaust.* New York: Macmillan, 1990.

*The Holocaust.* (video) New York: National Jewish Resource Center, 1984.

JOSEPHUS. *Complete Works.* Grand Rapids, Michigan2: Kregel, 1960.

LANADU, ELAINE. *Nazi War Criminals.* New York: Franklin Watts, 1990.

MELTZER, MILTON. *Never to Forget: The Jews of the Holocaust.* New York: Harper and Row, 1976.

PERLMAN, MOSHE. *The Capture and Trial of Adolf Eichmann.* New York: Simon & Schuster, 1963.

RABINOWITZ, DOROTHY. *About the Holocaust.* New York: American Jewish Committee, 1979.

ROTH, JOHN K. *A Consuming Fire.* Prologue by Elie Wiesel. Atlanta: John Knox Press, 1979.

SCHOENBERNER, GERHARD. *The Yellow Star.* New York: Bantam, 1973.

WHEAL, ELIZABETH-ANNE, STEPHEN POPE, and JAMES TAYLOR. *Encyclopedia of the Second World War.* Edison, N. J.: Castle, 1989.

ZENTNER, CHRISTIAN, and FRIEDEMANN BEDURDTIF, eds. *The Encyclopedia of the Third Reich.* New York: Macmillan, 1991.

ZISENWINE, DAVID W. *Anti-Semitism in Europe: Sources of the Holocaust.* New York: Behrman House, 1976.

**NOTES**